KILLER MEMORY

JEANNIE ROUSSEAU: A TRUE WWII FEMALE SPY STORY

JO DUVAL

CONTENTS

Introduction   vii

1. ESPIONAGE IN WARTIME   1
   How Espionage Was Used in Previous Wars   2
   The Value of Spies   7

2. THE INVASION AND OCCUPATION OF FRANCE   13
   Prelude to 1940   13
   The Beginning of the Vichy Government   21
   Life Under Occupation   23

3. THE FRENCH RESISTANCE   31
   The Formation of the French Resistance   33
   A Government in Exile   40

4. LIKE FATHER, LIKE DAUGHTER   45
   Earliest Spy Work   45
   Into the Lion's Den   48

5. THE GERMAN ROCKET PROGRAMME   53
   Nazi Wonder Weapons   53
   Hitler Has Lift-off   57
   The French Resistance vs. The Rocket Sites   58

6. ROUSSEAU SPIES ON THE ROCKETS   61

7. THE RAID ON PEENEMÜNDE   65
   Operation Hydra   65
   The Impact of Operation Hydra on the War   68

8. A HARROWING ESCAPE   71
   Amniarix: From Spy to Prisoner   72
   A Negotiated Release   78

9. JEANNIE'S LIFE AFTER THE WAR   81

Conclusion   85
References   91
About the Author   103

Those who worked underground in constant fear—fear of the unspeakable—were prompted by the inner obligation to participate in the struggle; almost powerless, they sensed they could listen and observe. . . . It is not easy to depict the lonesomeness, the chilling fear, the unending waiting, the frustration of not knowing whether the dangerously obtained information would be passed on—or passed on in time—recognized as vital in the maze of the couriers.

–Jeannie Rousseau

INTRODUCTION

A wise and brave woman once said, "Resistance is a state of mind. We can exercise it at any moment." So, who was this remarkable woman? Why, she was none other than Jeannie Rousseau–World War II spy. Of course, many spies are recognized for their hard work during World War II. Yet there are very few people aware of Jeannie Rousseau's efforts to bring down the German Rocket Programme.

It's no surprise that Jeannie's work has gone under the radar for as long as it has. After all, that was how she preferred to work. Working under code names and aliases, staying off the grid was what kept her alive. After the war, she lived in the shadows as she ducked reporters and historians. People wanted to hear her spy stories, but she wanted to move on with her life. It was not until 1998 that she agreed to sit down with a journalist and tell her story. That historic interview with *The Washington Post* was the only featured article that she took part in, and it was because *she* got to tell her story.

The journalist, David Ignatius, asked her why she had never shared her story before. To which she answered, "After the war, the curtain came down on my memories. What I did was so little. Others did so much more. I was one small stone." (Ignatius, 1998). Ignatius went on to compare Jeannie to many known 'genuine' heroes, people that would often disregard their work as an embarrassment rather than an accomplishment. By doing a quick internet search, there is little to find about Jeannie's time after the war. She is nowhere to be found on lists of influential women from history. It's hard not to think that maybe, just maybe, that is how she wanted it to be. She believed that what she did was not substantial, so she kept those details to herself. In Jeannie Rousseau's mind, she was simply a common French girl who was doing her job.

Was it true? Was Jeannie Rousseau just an ordinary run-of-the-mill French girl? And if that were the case, she obviously could not have been a major threat to the German forces or any of Hilter's plans. Right? Maybe it was the way that her eyes sparkled when she talked about science or how her smile captivated anyone she spoke to that drew the Nazi soldiers to her. Or maybe it was the way that she translated German for them, in a manner so perfect that nobody would dare question her. A girl that was this sweet and willing to help obviously could not be considered a serious threat. Or could she?

Just a Common French Girl?

Jeannie Rousseau appeared to be just an ordinary French girl. However, she was anything but. She was brilliant, graduating at the top of her class at an elite institution that has been accredited for creating some of the most intellectual government leaders and scientists. Her talented ear for translating foreign languages, unassuming nature, and pretty face made it easy for her to break into the spy world. She did not mind taking advantage of the fact that men saw her as an oblivious girl with good looks or that they did not take her seriously. Their ignorance only made it easier for her to make friends within the German ranks and get invited to places that most spies could only dream of.

After all, espionage was considered a male-dominated game throughout the history of war. Men had the physical strength, the expertise, and when they said something, they were not brushed off. Men did not have to worry about being seen as "domesticated" or "the gentler sex". A man's role was to be the breadwinner and protect his family, while women were expected to take care of the house, make dinner, and tend to the children. The male counterpart did not have to worry about gender bias in a bureaucratic system. They were free to dig in and get their hands dirty. While all of this may be true, men often forget about one fact–women will always find a way to do it better.

Men Do it Well, Women Do it Better

In Marcus Binney's book *The Women Who Lived for Danger*, a British spy trainer named Leslie Fernandez explained why women were better spies than men. "The girls were good at role-playing. Survival did not just require physical strength but the ability to live a cover story—which women could excel at" (Binney, 2004). In other words, the women may have done a great job at playing the role of the maid or the cook. But their expertise in that role allowed them to get close enough to the soldiers so they could listen to secret conversations. The non-threatening housewife that no one thought twice about as she hung her wet laundry out on the clothesline was actually sending a secret message or signaling to other agents.

The former head of the M15 intelligence organization, Dame Stella Rimington, gave multiple reasons why women were amazing at espionage work. She stated that women are better at listening and empathizing than men. These two qualities help build a trusting relationship with their target, allowing the person to let down their guard and start talking. Women are also better at keeping their cool during a heated situation while maintaining a balance of intelligence and common sense. They are less likely to go off the rails when a wrench is thrown in their plans and think rationally about handling the situation. Last but certainly not least, women are relentless, especially when it comes to protecting other people.

All of these qualities that make an excellent spy, male or female, could be found in Jeannie Rousseau. She listened to what the Nazi soldiers said and empathized with them. She gained their trust, and the German soldiers started pouring out their secrets. When she was arrested and later thrown into multiple concentration camps, she stayed calm and used her wit to stay two steps ahead of the guards. Most importantly, she was relentless and refused to stop working until her job was done. Jeannie Rousseau is the picture-perfect example of what a female spy was and should be.

ESPIONAGE IN WARTIME

What exactly is a spy? Is it the man listening to conversations from the next room and looking through trash cans for information to steal about his enemy? Is it the femme fatale, seducing men and giving away the details they earned during pillow talk? Could it possibly be both? The answer is yes–and no. The technical definition of a spy is a person who secretly collects and reports information on the activities, movements, and plans of an enemy or competitor (Merriam-Webster, n.d.). In other words, while these examples are considered the work of a spy, someone that is working in espionage is usually much more covert. They were not the men wearing the trench coat carrying magnifying glasses that one may see in old movies. They were the housewives and maids cleaning the house and taking care of the children as they passed along messages to other agents.

Both Allied and Axis forces used spies and espionage rings during World War II in order to gain intelligence and secretive plans of their enemy. However, this is not the first occasion that espionage was used. Espionage was used long before World War II, even going as far back as the Revolutionary War. In fact, one

British Army Officer has said that "George Washington didn't really outfight the British; he had simply outspied them" (Gruber, 2021). The year was 1775 when General George Washington, who was in charge of the Continental Army at that time, created the Army's first intelligence organization. He sent some of his men back to Boston to keep an eye on any movements by the British armed forces. The information that they gathered and brought back to him was then used to deceive the British troops and later raid their encampments.

HOW ESPIONAGE WAS USED IN PREVIOUS WARS

Austria and Hungary were the first countries to start a Secret Service, simultaneously creating their organizations in 1850. Twenty-one years later, France followed suit and created its own in 1871. Shortly behind them were Germany and Italy. Britain was the last one to jump on the bandwagon, finally creating its Secret Service organization in 1909 (AUI, 1996).

From the beginning of the 19th century, it was the military and naval officers that played the critical role of gathering intelligence. However, these soldiers had one golden rule that they were required to follow. Under no circumstance were they allowed to spy on their own country. But, of course, there is not a story in history that doesn't include a few rule-breakers. While many followed this rule and recruited agents to spy on their surrounding countries, there were a few that did not. They took the risk, staying in their home country, and gathered information anyway.

Both sides used different tactics to uncover secrets about the enemy during World War I, hoping that the information would give their side an advantage over the other. Most of this work included the cracking of codes that were sent back and forth by telegraph or radio. Cryptographers would work mercilessly to create unique secret codes that would reach their intended destination safely and securely. Then, they would work on cracking the messages that were intercepted from the enemy.

Sending encrypted codes was not the only way to get a message across. Sometimes spies had to get creative with the stolen information. In 1915, two Dutch spies were tried and executed after being caught with cigars that looked a little suspicious. British soldiers held the men posing as cigar importers as they sliced open their tobacco-filled cargo and found secret messages. An ordinary can of food supposedly holding an ox tongue was sent to Jack Shaw, a British Lieutenant being held in a German camp. Inside the can held a compass, wire cutters, and a folded map to help the man arrange a mass escape. Small weights had been added to the can so it would be the proper weight, and would not catch the attention of the German soldiers. One of the most popular ways to get messages to the target safely was by carrier pigeon. Messenger pigeons were used by both German and British armies, and they used thousands of them. The information would be written on rice paper and rolled to fit into a small capsule that was attached to the bird's leg (Kindersley, 2019).

Before World War I, there was little use for spies, and the Secret Service held no significant meaning in America. That is until espionage became the main reason that the United States entered the war. British Intelligence had decrypted a message from Germany that was meant for Mexico and presented it to President Woodrow Wilson. The telegram, which later came to be known as the Zimmerman Telegram, was sent on January 12, 1917, by the German Minister Arthur Zimmerman to the German representatives in Mexico. The diplomats were to approach the Mexican government and offer them a generous amount of financial support if Mexico joined them. If Mexico agreed to fight alongside them, they would ensure that the country would get Arizona, New Mexico, and Texas back when the war was over. He had also unveiled Germany's plan of a submarine attack on February 1, that would push America into conflict with them (Bomboy, 2022). Still upset and believing that the three states that America now owned had been illegally seized, Mexican President Venustiano Carranza ordered his government to study the German's offer. He considered the proposal but decided to decline their offer, but he would keep their offer reserved if America were ever to invade his country's minefields (Peck, 2017).

Axis Espionage

The Axis forces took their spy work to a whole new level when they organized their espionage operations. After the 1940 armistice, the Nazis chose to use espionage to keep track of France and ensure they were following their terms. The French were used to the inspections that were announced ahead of time, making sure that they were on their best behavior and following the rules. However, using undercover spies was useful when it came to keeping an eye out for breaches when the citizens had let their guards down.

The undercover spies also made it possible to flow smoothly through the bureaucratic channels, infiltrating meetings and sending the plans back to Germany before the French could realize what was going on. Joseph Barthélemy, Vichy's Justice Minister, recalled in his memoirs that within minutes of each cabinet meeting, the Germans knew everything that was said and discussed.

The Germans would go on to infiltrate France's military, youth groups, and police force. The spies that infiltrated the police force would act as bodyguards for the three leading officials in the state: Francois Darlan, Marshal Philippe Pétain, and Laval. Germany was not a stranger to using women as spies, often sending them in to seduce officials and French diplomats. One woman, in particular, was very good at her job and was responsible for getting the German spies hired to the police force. She was the sister of the police inspector that was responsible for guarding Francois Darlan. She was also the mistress of Vichy's head of the Gestapo delegation, Hugo Geissler (Kitson, 2008, pp. 7–25).

The infiltration of the military, paramilitary, police force, and youth groups had a significant purpose. They were the eyes and ears on the streets of France, watching and listening to the surrounding areas and making sure that France was not rebuilding its armed forces. German Secret Service agents were given orders to live in the unoccupied southern territories. They would be responsible for keeping the German administration safe from being infiltrated by Allie spies.

German SS agents would often go as far as pretending to be members of the French Resistance, pretending to hate the Nazi regime and everything they stood for. These agents found their position within the Resistance groups to be beneficial, as they gathered and extracted information from members that were willing to give it up. These spies were eventually sought out and arrested and would usually claim that they worked for the British before finally telling the truth. One of these German spies, a man named Edouard Buch, recalls what the Germans trained him to tell the Resistance members in the event that he was arrested. He stated, "I was never supposed to divulge the mission I was charged with, and in the event of interrogation by the French police, I was to try to convince them that my presence in the free zone was solely motivated by my desire to get away from the Germans" (Kitson, 2008, pp. 7–25).

Duquesne Spy Ring was an outfit that had infiltrated the United States. The government found a total of 33 Nazi spies that were sent to spy on American soil. On December 13, 1941, all of them pled guilty and were convicted of their crimes, including the group's ringleader, Fritz Duquesne. The man who brought the spy ring down was a double agent by a naturalized German immigrant by the name of William Sebold. He had been recruited by the Nazis when he returned to his native country of Germany to visit his mother. The Nazis learned of Sebold's low-ranking job in the aircraft industry and believed that having a spy in Manhattan working for them would ensure that they would be informed of any attacks headed their way.

The head of Wehrmacht's espionage ring, Colonel Nikolaus Ritter, already had information and blueprints regarding an important development in a military project that was going on in the United States. German immigrant and Nazi supporter Hermann Lang had been working as a spy for the Germans since 1937 and was employed at a factory in New York. Unbeknownst to the Norden factory, he was working for; Lang had been copying blueprints and handing them over to Ritter willingly (Connelly, 2014).

Ritter had a man to give up information, but he also needed one to receive such information, only to pass it along to other secret spies in Manhattan. Sebold was coerced to take the position and contacted the U.S. Consulate to tell them about the Colonel's forceful invitation. FBI agents met Sebold when his boat docked in Washington, and he was taken to their headquarters, where he told them everything that he knew. He told them about the offer to work as a spy for the Nazis as well as all of the spies that were already working on American soil. After years of Sebold's hard work to uncover these secretive spy rings, the men and women were pulled out of their beds and arrested on June 28, 1941 (Connelly, 2014).

Allies Espionage

The United States used espionage in other ways during World War II by spying on their own allies. They intercepted secret diplomatic messages and took the time to break encrypted codes. Of course, it goes without saying that Allied intelligence could not have gotten far without the use of the Enigma Machine. The

British Intelligence's ability to intercept, interfere, translate, and decipher the codes gave them a major advantage over the Germans. Although, having this advantage sometimes had its downside. Besides the intelligence practices that it required to operate the machine, the Allied commanders became over-reliant on it.

During Operation Fortitude, the British would crack the German enigma codes. These codes would give away the locations, arrival times, and how many of their men would be parachuted in. Once the soldiers landed, they were captured and arrested by the British MI-5 team. Unfortunately, these German soldiers were not well-trained in how to land unseen or misconstruing information during an interrogation. They would be given two options during their interrogation: agree to work for the British or be executed. It was an obvious choice for many of the soldiers, as they opted to take the first option. However, quite a few opted for the latter, pledging allegiance to their home country before they were executed by a military firing squad.

One of the best examples of the Allied forces' espionage practices would be Winston Churchill's Special Operations Executive or SOE. While they performed many operations within Europe, Denmark was where the intelligence group truly shined. The organization performed over 1,000 operations in the country alone, ranging from rescuing Jews from being persecuted to sabotaging German transport paths by detonating bombs underneath bridges.

THE VALUE OF SPIES

Wars that were fought before intelligence organizations came to fruition terrified the armed forces. Soldiers going in blind to war-ridden countries without a clue as to what their enemies were planning was considered extremely dangerous. However, a spy hidden in plain sight, in an area that nobody would suspect, could give them an advantage. This tactic was the reason that spies like

Jeannie Rousseau were so successful. She often worked closely with the German soldiers and collected information right under their noses.

A well-placed spy could feed them information, like giving them reasons why the enemy was doing something, their objectives, and intentions, which would give them a view of specific reasoning and not just the time or location. Spies could intercept crucial intelligence information through wire-tapping and breaking the opposition's codes. They could also develop close contacts so that they could gather information that would work in the best interest of their country. Not only could spies feed their host country with information, but they could also leak misinformation to the opposing country while keeping an eye on political extremists and suspicious foreign nationals.

The spy's ability to pass on data regarding where troops were headed, how many soldiers were in the platoons and the condition of the men was of utmost value to war generals. This information could make a world of difference when it came to the likelihood of whether the army could win or lose the battle. It could allow the generals to know when and where they needed to plan an attack to guarantee a win, as well as when they needed to retreat.

The practice of spies was useful and successful, especially when it came to catching their men double-crossing their own country. One of Washington's espionage rings, the Culper Spy Rings, is believed to be responsible for catching Benedict Arnold's betrayal. By discovering Arnold's treason with Britain, they also indirectly exposed the head of Britain's secret service and Benedict's partner, Major John André. While Arnold managed to escape to England, where he would later lead the British troops in Connecticut and Virginia, André was hanged for his crime of being a spy (History, 2009).

Another example would be the Dutch-born dancer, Mata Hari. She came to Paris in 1905 as a performer in Asian-inspired dance, claiming that she was raised in a sacred temple in India where she was taught to dance by a priestess. Except, Mata Hari was actually Margaretha Geertruida Zelle, a small-town girl from Holland. She danced in opera houses and dance halls, with most of her shows included her stripping nude while she cataloged a long list of lovers of high-ranking government officials. Hari was eventually arrested by the French authorities in February 1917, accused of giving away Allies' war secrets that cost many soldiers their lives. They had evidence that she was working as a German spy, but she had proved to be ineffective and had not given them any valuable information. Hari was blindfolded and executed by a French firing squad six months later (History, 2018b). While her trial was filled with circumstantial evidence and bias, her story became a cautionary tale among female spies.

Women Working Behind Enemy Lines

When World War II began, women were quick to step into the men's shoes and take over the workplace. With many of the men being called to the battlefield, they had no choice but to step in. They worked in factories, built boats, flew airplanes, and drove fire trucks. According to historian Kevin Hymel, "With their men away, women became more self-sufficient. Many brought tools home from work and used them on their own home repairs. They took on domestic roles they never had before" (McDermott, 2018). It was estimated that nearly 6 million women stepped into the work-force during World War II, taking on jobs that were not usually suited for women.

It was then that intelligence agencies realized women could be a valuable asset to the spy world as well. Noticing that women were rarely stopped or questioned at checkpoints, they could carry out tasks much easier than men. For whatever reason, women were considered less of a threat. Maybe it was their femininity that helped play on the stereotypes and egos of the soldiers. It was understandable how their frail and damsel in distress personas could get them out of sticky situations, which would not work for a man. Not to mention that many of the women were more resourceful and inventive than the male agents.

The Nazis fell into this stereotypical role, and it very well could be one of the many reasons the Germans lost the war. The "Superior" race did not think very much of women. They considered females less dangerous, nowhere near as vengeful, dumber, and weaker than men. Their force-fed propaganda depicted women as loving mothers, living a docile life with multiple children and tending to their husbands. It's no wonder that they had a hard time considering a woman could be a spy or member of the Resistance.

The SOE, sometimes referred to as "Churchill's Secret Army," had 39 female agents working for them that had to be deployed out into the field after D-Day. The women could blend in with society and speak perfect French to evade any suspicion. Each female agent knew how to hold their own when out in the field. They were trained with specialist skills and knew how to pick locks, break into homes, and maintain their cover story if someone caught them.

Some female spies were trained how to shoot a gun, handle explosives, organize supply drops, endure an interrogation, memorize lists of complex codes, and be in charge of multiple men. Others used their gifts of persuasion, looks, charm, and intelligence to become one with the enemy crowd. Jeannie Rousseau was the latter of the two.

Women were not only considered a value in the world of espionage; they were also an inspiration to the future generations of girls who wanted to serve their country. In Jeannie Rousseau's case, her inspiration was a World War I spy by the name of Louise de Bettignies. Louise was a French girl that came from a privileged family. She was a skilled linguist that spoke German and English fluently. When her city came under bombardment in October of 1914, she helped supply the soldiers in her city with food and ammunition. While helping out the men defending her country, Louise used her translation skills to help the wounded and dying German soldiers write letters to their families.

The German forces eventually took over her hometown of Lille, and that is when the helpful girl turned into a spy. Working under the name of Alice Dubois, Louise worked for the M16 and the British army. For nine months, de Bettignies saved thousands of British soldiers' lives and supplied the M16 intelligence with vital information. Information that she had gathered while traveling through the occupied Belgium and France, her small and ill appearance diverting any suspicion of her being a spy. Louise was eventually arrested in October of 1915 and spent the next three years working in labor camps. She would eventually succumb to infected abscesses in 1918 due to her preexisting health conditions and the poor sanitary conditions of the prisons.

2

THE INVASION AND OCCUPATION
OF FRANCE

The Germans were victorious in their invasion of France between the months of May and June of 1940, sending shockwaves around the world. After all, France had one of the biggest and most powerful armies in Western Europe, playing a large part in their victory during the First World War. Surely, they should have been able to hold out on their own. If not, then possibly turn back the German tide and get them to surrender. Unfortunately, that would not happen. The Allied forces in France would be defeated early on and placed Nazi Germany and the Axis forces in complete control of Western Europe until 1944.

PRELUDE TO 1940

The deep-rooted resentment and rivalry between the two countries played a large part in Germany's invasion of France. Both of them had considerably the greatest amount of military powers on the European continent, and they shared a border. Gripped within a power struggle, this would not be the first time that Germany and

France found themselves in armed conflict before the 1940 invasion. Before the beginning of World War II, France had nearly 1 million soldiers and over 5 million that had been trained and placed on the back burner in preparation for another war. Besides the trained troops, the French army also had 3,000 tanks at their disposal. The tanks' firepower ability was considered highly superior to those owned by the Germans. Unfortunately, the Hilter had built up their armed forces the first 17 months after becoming Chancellor as he prepared for the invasion. In less than a year and a half, the Fuhrer had recruited enough men for 36 divisions. His army quickly grew from 2.5 million Nazi soldiers to 13.6 million (Shepherd, 2016).

The precursor to all of this madness began in the year 1914. Germany had a grand plan to invade France in order to knock them out of the growing global conflict that would become the First World War. Advancing toward Paris as quickly as they could, the Germans drove through Belgium and the Netherlands. They hoped that if the French army would quickly surrender, they could focus all of their resources and energy on the Russian Empire. Instead, the German army was held in a standoff that would last four years by the French, British, Belgian, Dutch, and colonial forces (Brereton Greenhous & Tattrie, 2018). After a failed submarine attack, Germany ultimately surrendered to the Allied forces. The loss would go down in history with the signing of the Treaty of Versailles in November 1918.

After the loss, the German Empire was in ruins, and the victorious powers grew larger. Germany slowly began to transition into a Republican political system. However, the country's rebirth moved slowly because of the strict restrictions placed on them by the treaty. First of all, they had to take responsibility for starting the war. Secondly, their army had been restricted to the limit of 100,000 men. The treaty had even put stipulations on what kind of soldiers Germany could have. The country could no longer force its men to enlist in the armed forces. The soldiers had to volunteer to join willingly. Their army could also not be in possession of any submarines, armored tanks, or aircraft, and they were only allowed to have six naval battleships. The country's funds would be tied up in reparations, paying for the damage that the war caused, and their territories would be split up and given to other countries (Walsh, n.d.).

Germany had been undeniably defeated. Even though no German territory had been captured by any of their enemies, the treaty had cost them 10% of their lands and territories. The German government was unable to accept this fact. Humiliated about everything their country had lost, protestors filled the streets of the German Parliament. This humiliation would serve as the main course from which the Nazi politicians of the 1920s and 1930s, many of whom had themselves served in the First World War, would draw their strength. Nazi leader, Adolf Hitler, would not less this stand and set his sights on expansion. He fed his fellow Nazis promises of German resurgence, placing the blame on Germany's Jewish population for the loss of the war. The beginning of his propaganda attack began as Hitler spread the rumor of how the Jews had sat at home while the soldiers on the front lines fought valiantly.

Meanwhile in Brittany

Life was not chaotic for everyone after the end of the First World War. The woman who would come to be known for her amazing spy work in order to help bring down the Nazi regime in years to come was born Jeannie Yvonne Ghislaine Rousseau on April 1, 1919—born in Saint-Brieuc, in Brittany, located in the northwestern region of France. Jeannie was an only child to parents, Jean Rousseau and Marie Le Charpentier. Her father was a World War One veteran that became a Senior official with the foreign ministry. When describing her father's involvement in the war, Jeannie stated he was "not a hero, but solid" (Ignatius, 1998). After he retired, Jean would become the mayor of the 17th Arrondissement in Paris. During his time in office, the family would deal with the upcoming war as Germany planned its revenge.

The Invasion of France

Hitler now had a larger and stronger army, and he was ready to kick off the war in Europe with the swift invasion of Poland and the Soviet Union in September of 1939. Sandwiched between the Soviets to the east and the Germans to the west, the Polish forces did their best to resist the attackers, but it did not work as well as they had hoped. Their attackers were far more advanced than they were, and they were officially occupied by October of 1939 (History, 2009). From there, the German Reich moved onto Czechoslovakia and Austria, gaining control of the countries as quickly as they had with Poland. The Soviet Union saw that they were easily outnumbered and signed a nonaggression pact with the determined occupiers. With the Soviets out of the way, the Nazi state was free to turn its attention to the West to begin planning the next phase in their conquest of Europe–setting their sights directly on France.

The French and British governments were guarantors of Polish sovereignty. With the shocking invasion of Poland by the Germans, a French declaration of war came along with it. The next few months would be widely dubbed "the Phoney War," littered with sparse amounts of military action. Germany took this time to refit and regroup their forces for the impending invasion of France, while the French planned and prepared their defense strategies.

The French armed forces began to construct a series of fortifications and emplacements along their shared border with Germany, known as the Maginot line. The fortifications were built with the sole intention of serving as a deterrent to any direct attacks. The generals hoped that line of defense would push the German forces north through Belgium, where the French were ready to meet them (Donnell & Spedaliere, 2017). Instead, the German Army had an alternative plan. Unbeknownst to the French Military, the Germans developed their own warfare breakthrough consisting of fast-paced armored tanks.

Meanwhile in Paris

The Germans were not the only ones making major developments. Jeannie had enrolled in the Finance course at the elite French University, Sciences Po. Throughout her time there, she excelled in all of her classes, ranging from the study of insurance to social economics. Rousseau's professors had nothing but nice things to say about her work and character inside the classroom. Her level of intelligence was quickly noticed by all of her professors, especially her Social Economics teacher, Pierre Waline. Professor Waline cited a specific set of oral presentations that Rousseau had completed in 1938, stating, "One was good, the other almost too good. Speaks easily, a little too fast. Intelligent student, evidently more at ease in oral presentations than in written work" (SciencesPo, 2018).

Her friend, Claude de Granrut, remembers how much Jeannie loved how Sciences Po provided a window that gave her a view of foreign cultures. Granrut met Rousseau in 1946 and has always appreciated Jeannie for convincing him to apply to Sciences Po. He has been quoted as saying, "She had loved the constant emphasis on cultural exchange and had made some very dear friends there" (SciencesPo, 2018). The German and English courses that the

University provided helped her to discover that she had an ear for many foreign languages. Little did Miss Rousseau know that her interpretation skills would act as a compass for her future work as a spy. In 1939, at the young and vibrant age of twenty, Jeannie graduated at the top of her class.

A Change in Government

It was in May of 1940 that the French parliament made a major change, placing their government in new hands. Paul Reynard had replaced Edouard Daladier as the Prime Minister, and the Phoney War ended soon after. The ending was sudden, but not completely unexpected. The sudden change in plans only occurred when the German forces invaded Norway. The static defenses of the Maginot Line had been ineffective against the occupying troops, and the French forces were outsmarted thanks to those advanced tanks. The German armored columns had found a gap in the line at the Ardennes forest. If the tanks had been the same as they had been used during the First World War, they would not have been able to make it through the gap. But with the new technology, the Ardennes forest was the equivalent of a minor speed bump.

The French force's defense line had been completely side-stepped, allowing the German forces to make rapid advances through France. Now they only had one obstacle in front of them, the Allied troops waiting for them along the coastline. The events that would take place during the months of May and June 1940 would become known as "Operation Dynamo". The operation all began when one German troop swept through Belgium and Holland to head into northern France, forcing the Allied troops to move north in order to meet them. Another much larger and stronger German troop pushed through Luxembourg, cutting across the northern part of France to get to the coast. The men were heavily armed, and they moved quickly through the coast, allowing them to trap the Allied soldiers. Over the next two weeks, the occupying forces invaded the city of Boulogne and Calais.

Meanwhile, the remainders of the French Army and the two British divisions were desperate as they tried to defend themselves in Somme and Aisne. Their air forces had lost a lot of airmen thanks to the German's fighter jets, telling the French government that a full invasion of the country was imminent. With the threat of a Paris occupation, the French government was forced to pack up and relocate to Bordeaux. On July 10, the newly-relocated French government declared that Paris was an open city. They hoped that by claiming the city was now open would protect it from any more attacks and bombings. The parliament had already seen what the Axis powers had done in Warsaw and Antwerp, leaving the cities in complete shambles. The Allied forces attempted to hold back the advance on Paris for four days, but they were unsuccessful. On June 14, German forces successfully entered and took over the City of Lights (History, 2021).

The battle for France continued well into the next month. By the end of the battle, the French forces had already lost more men than they could possibly replace, and the Germans made significant gains in invading many European cities. The only way that they could try to recoup their losses and save the rest of the country from a complete takeover was to seek an Armistice. The Maginot Line and other fortification tactics had become ineffective. The bulk of their weapons had been destroyed, and they had lost over 92,000 of their soldiers. Paris had found itself in German hands, and the French cabinet saw a shift in leadership after the disastrous defeat. Reviewing their options, the French leaders did not see any other way to salvage what was left if they did not go ahead with the signing.

However, the decision to sign the armistice was not unanimous among all French government officials. French Prime Minister Paul Reynaud felt that the French should keep fighting, but other officials felt the opposite. The parliament took a vote, and the results came to 569 votes for abandoning the former Third Republic government to 80 votes for staying and fighting. As a sign of protest against the Armistice, Reynaud resigned as leader of the nation. His position was promptly filled by First World War general and national hero, Philippe Pétain. It was only two months prior to receiving his new position as the French Prime Minister that Pétain had been appointed as France's vice premier. His job description required him to boost the country's morale despite the Nazi invasion; instead, he arranged the signing of an armistice. He proudly declared his reasoning for the arrangement, stating that it was "better to be a Nazi province. At least we know what that means" (Kaiser, 2015). Almost immediately after the vote to sign the armistice and give Pétain full control, the parliament was dissolved. The new prime minister would now be the only bureaucratic system of checks and balances that could enact any type of policy.

Hitler's Attempt to Remake History

As a symbolic gesture of spite, Adolf Hitler organized the armistice signing to take place in the very same railcar that the First World War armistice was signed, signaling Germany's surrender. He even went as far as having the railcar, known as the *Compiègne Wagon*, removed from a museum exhibit and placing it in the exact same location that the first armistice was signed. The Führer appeared to use this act of petty revenge to repeat how World War I should have gone. Facing the French delegates as they listened to the preamble of the armistice, he sat in the same chair that Marshal Ferdinand Foch had sat in when Germany surrendered in 1918. Following Foch's lead in a calculated move to show his disgust for the French delegates, Hitler excused himself from the railcar carriage and left the negotiations up to General Wilhelm Keitel, the Chief of the high commanding officers. After a full day of negotiations, France was officially under German occupation. The French signed the armistice on June 22, 1940, but it would not go into full effect until June 25.

THE BEGINNING OF THE VICHY GOVERNMENT

Less than a month after signing the armistice with Germany, General Pétain became the leader of the collaborationist French government Vichy France. He took office as the "chief of state" and soon started to collaborate with the Nazis. Pétain made his first order as the leader of the new Vichy government– arresting former Prime Minister Reynaud. Paul Reynaud, along with two other former Prime Ministers, Edouard Daladier, and Leon Blum, were later tried for betraying their country in February 1942. All three men were found guilty of these treacherous crimes and handed over to the Germans, who kept them prisoner, until 1945. In response to the trial of his comrade, Charles de Gaulle challenged the authority of Petain and his Vichy Regime, making the public claim that the French Government was in exile.

A Paper with a Purpose

The 1940 armistice's stipulations were crystal clear, leaving no room for miscommunication between the two countries. France was to be divided into two defined zones: one zone being heavily occupied by German forces. What was leftover would be considered unoccupied and free under French rule. The occupied region of the country would include the northern portion of the country and the Atlantic coast until it reached the western border of the Pyrenees. This left only two-fifths of the country's territory unoccupied. The French also needed to neutralize their air force and navy, but the armed forces were not required to be given to the Germans. Despite being able to keep the armed forces, the unoccupied areas of France were ordered to hand over any heavy artillery weapons, and they had to be in good condition.

Desperate to make some type of stand, the French officials did not leave the rail car without contesting some stipulations to the agreement. They disagreed with the mandatory turnover of German refugees to the authorities, the barrier that established the boundaries, and that the terms of the agreement could be modified to reach the Italian's demands at any time. Surprisingly, the Italians were generous with their terms, stating that they would only occupy the small frontier that they had already occupied since June 20. In return for their generosity, the Italians demanded that France demilitarize their naval bases in Tunisia and Algeria (Britannica, 2022). Once that task was completed, the Italians could go through with their own plans.

Did Pétain Become a Fascist collaborator with the Nazis?

Historians believe that the initial reason the parliament threw in the towel was the humiliation that they endured due to the German forces being able to invade them so quickly. They looked anywhere they could for a scapegoat, using Jews, communists, and socialists to place the blame on. However, the new government's treatment of these groups, particularly the Jews, did not necessarily make them a fascist regime. Historian Robert Paxton substantiated this claim, stating, "I think the best term for them is authoritarian. It doesn't act like a fascist regime because traditionally, elites have to give way, and in authoritarianism, they retain power. But all the foreign Jews were put into camps, they cracked down on dissent, and it was in some ways increasingly a police state" (Paxton, 2001).

The Vichy Regime has been seen as a lesser of two evils, but it is understandable how it could be seen as a collaborator with the Third Reich. Before the Nazis demanded their participation in their persecution of the Jews and their anti-Semitic policies, French officials had already started to seize the Jew's property and remove them from any civil service. It is a known fact that before Hitler created his oppressing laws, the French police were already willing participants in the deportation of Jewish families. At no time were the Nazis twisting their arms. The French police had committed most of the arrests of their own volition. All in all, the Vichy regime was solely responsible for the deportation of 75,721 French citizens and Jewish refugees, sending them to their death in concentration camps (Boissoneault, 2017).

LIFE UNDER OCCUPATION

The Vichy Regime may have technically had control of France and its overseas colonies, but the government only had a small sway over the southern and eastern half of the nation. The rest of the country, including Paris, was under direct German occupation regardless of the Vichy government's authority. As soon as Vichy France was established, they began their collaborationist activities. French police officers were independent of the Nazis but were still required to act in accordance with their policies. One of these policies included the rounding up of French Jews, communists, partisans, political opponents, and anyone else the conservative leaders wanted to be eliminated or seen as a threat.

These round-ups only furthered the publics' perception of Pétain and his voluntary collaboration with the Nazis. The active and independent actions of the French authorities only served as an example of these beliefs. In the book *When Paris went dark: the City of Light under German occupation*, author Ronald Rosbottom provided the explanation regarding why the French civilians held so much hostility toward their new leader. He stated, "Indeed, there is no way the Germans could have succeeded as well as they did in rounding up these "illegals" if it had not been for the help of the local police forces. The Germans quite simply did not have enough personnel to track and keep files on Jews or plan and carry out raids, arrests, and incarcerations. Nor did they know as intimately the labyrinth that was the city of Paris." (Rosbottom, 2015, 14.85).

Under the Nazi's Control

Initially, the people of France supported the choice to sign the armistice, especially after they considered what could happen to their country if France had decided to keep fighting. However, many of the citizens did not support the new policies that were being made by the Vichy state. Although the Vichy Regime was fundamentally opposed to the traditions of the French Republic, Pétain was still trying to realign societal views with a conservative version of their occupiers, whether the people of France wanted it or not. In response to the new government and the sequential German occupation, a considerable resistance movement was organized.

In the German-controlled northern sector of the country, the authority of the Vichy regime was being supported by tens of thousands of Gestapo security officers, police, and SS intelligence to cement their control of the French citizens. German signs were hung up all over Paris, Swastikas flew over national landmarks and monuments, and the civilians were pervasively and routinely watched by surveillance. French citizens were ordered to abide by an 8 p.m. curfew, requiring a pass if they wanted to go out at night. They were forcibly enlisted into the local war industries. The ones that were deemed 'undesirable' by the regime were forced into slave labor, many of them dying due to the unsafe work conditions or at the hands of the guards.

Rationing became a daily fact of life as resources were diverted to the war effort. The Nazi troops quickly confiscated large amounts of fuel and fertilizer and took farmers with them upon arrival. They also seized about 20% of the produce, half of the meat, and over 80% of the country's champagne (Moure, 2010). The government attempted to solve the difficulties caused by the seizing of their food by rationing out items like bread, meat, butter, and cooking oils in exchange for tickets. They also supplemented people with the items they would need to build a home garden. The cargo vessels and boats that the French relied on for importing and exporting goods were not allowed to leave the ports. This law had a negative impact on how the French could get the supplies they needed, leaving many families without essential supplies.

Not only rationing but the French civilians were held to an armistice condition that required them to pay for the German troops while they were on their soil. Paying for an army of over 300,000 occupiers would cost around 20 million *Reichsmark* per day. According to the American Historical Association, at that time, the currency exchange rate was 1 *Reichsmark* to 20 French francs (Occhino et al., 2008). It has been estimated that between the years of 1940 to 1944, the French handed over 479 billion francs to the Germans. Today that would be around $517 billion US dollars! The Occupied citizens of France could not afford these payments, and as a result, they could not afford the necessities. No necessities meant no food and high levels of malnutrition, particularly among the country's young children.

Hitler's Country of Degradation and Devalue

Massive propaganda efforts were launched in the hope of increasing the French's support for the Nazis' anti-communist, anti-Semitic, and anti-Allied beliefs. In an effort to push their views into the minds of the people, the only source of news that was allowed to be published for soldiers stationed in Paris and the population of the Occupied Zone was the *Pariser Zeitung*. The daily publication would range from 8 to 13 pages long and was written entirely in German and graciously included a one-page summary in French for the locals. All of the articles were extremely anti-British, including the daily cartoon section that depicted cruel caricatures of Britain leaders. Interestingly, the Vichy correspondents that wrote for the paper worked hard to point out similarities between the French and German cultures and how they complimented each other. The newspaper was to be flattery to the French and promotion of the Nazis' eventual final solution.

Night clubs took out advertisements, and France was presented as the ultimate vacation destination for the conquering German. The promotions made Paris look as if it would become a major recreation center for future German rulers. It also implied that France would be a helpful force in the New Order that was sure to come in Europe. The paper emphasized to the French that Paris' cultural life was flourishing as much as it had been before it was under Nazi control. French actors, singers, and writers were featured and praised as artists. The German authorities claimed credit for the rebirth of France's film industry, an industry that had been significantly suppressed and shut down when the country was first occupied.

In Vichy, France, the German presence was considerably less noticeable than in the Occupied Zone. However, there was no mistaking that the culture and policies of the Vichy government were parallel to the Nazis'. It left many wondering if the Nazis were using Petain and his newly established government as a puppet or if they were willingly collaborating with them.

German Oppression Tactics in Occupied France

When the Germans first arrived in France, it was reported that they had tried to be nice to the country's people. Jeannie Rousseau had once stated that the Germans were trying to show that they could work alongside the French, a collaboration of sorts. The *Pariser Zeitung* presented a united front between the two countries, filling the French people with hopes that the death toll would eventually stop rising. In time, that kindness ran out and turned to cruel brutality.

A forced labor policy was enacted not long into the occupation called the *Service du Travail Obligatoire*, or the Obligatory work service. The policy required French workers to be rounded up and transferred to Germany, usually against their will, to work for them (Vinen, 2006). Some of the workers would be sent to work camps that forced them to work on railroads, in factories, or work their fields. Some of them were sent to top-secret V-1 testing and launch sites, locations that Jeannie would uncover in the near future. This obligated work detail is also what would set Jeannie's resistance within the labor camps in motion.

Breaking Down the Enemy

Oppression and humiliation were not new tactics for the Nazi regime. The occupiers enjoyed using humiliation and oppressive techniques to not only degrade and devalue the French but also to reinforce the lesson that the civilians were much lower than they were on the racial hierarchy. The Nazis had three objectives when it came to their humiliation: remind the occupied citizens of the risks of opposing them, heighten the suffering of the Jews, and degrade the victims enough to put distance between them and the occupied. The German soldiers would single out one or two people in a group to be punished. Most of the cases were civilians involved in a "mixed-race" couple, usually "Aryans" who were dating or married to a Jew. If a Jewish person were to go to the French police to report something that happened to them, they were beaten, their head was shaved, and they were paraded through the streets wearing signs around their necks.

The Jews were not only humiliated individually but systematically. They were considered inferior and were to be excluded from any type of daily life. A curfew was imposed on them, and they were restricted from using certain shops and types of public transit. Public park benches and drinking fountains were labeled with "Only for Aryans" signs or with a "J" if they were allowed to use them. Jewish families were sent to live in ghettos. The degrading conditions of overcrowding, poor sanitation, and malnutrition were seen as punishment for being born the wrong race. The worst act of oppression toward the Jews and other French resisters is well known, the gas and execution chambers. The Nazis built one in Paris in the cellars of the Ministry of Aviation building.

While they worked on humiliating these people, the Nazis worked on attacking them from another angle–using propaganda. They hung posters meant to deceive the public, painting Germany as the victim. The only way that they could make it right was through the extermination of the Jews, or what was known as the "Final Solution". After forcing Jewish families to move into ghettos, the Nazis spread lies about how they spread diseases. They even went as far as hanging quarantine signs outside of the buildings, keeping non-Jewish civilians from entering the premises, and seeing the conditions the Jews were being forced to live in. A hoax was enacted and aimed toward disabled veterans, elderly Jews, and prominent artists and musicians. They were to be sent to a 'retirement community' where they could live out the rest of their days in peace called *Theresienstadt*. In reality, *Theresienstadt* was a prison camp in the Czech province of Bohemia. The Nazi regime's propaganda tactics were merciless and were put in place until the end of the war.

The Germans may have gotten away with their oppression and humiliation for a while, but there was an uprising building. It was not a large military group, but rather small groups of people that would band together to resist. The Germans knew that strength came in numbers, and this group was quickly getting bigger and stronger by the day.

3

THE FRENCH RESISTANCE

Two months later, after the Germans made their way to France, a call to arms was sent over the radio waves from the BBC Broadcasting company in London. Two-Star General Charles de Gaulle's voice was sent over those airwaves in a move that would later be considered the first step in forming the French Resistance. De Gaulle was not a well-known name among the people of France, but he held a type of notoriety with the French military and the country's leaders. He was the man that had appointed Paul Reynaud as the Prime Minister when Germany invaded France. The choice proved to be a political failure, seeing as Raynaud chose to bring Generals Petain and Weygand into the cabinet. This move showed de Gaulle that the French leaders no longer had any fight left in them, and he, in turn, chose exile.

He fled to London with only a few supporters behind him. In London, de Gaulle isolated himself and built up his strength. While he lay dormant, Petain was accidentally adding to his prestige as an opposing and resistant force. First, the new leader of the Vichy government publicly stripped de Gaulle of his military rank and made him the focus of a smear campaign. Government officials went as far as hanging posters representing de Gaulle as a tall shadowy figure hiding behind a microphone and surrounded by Jews. Vichy's efforts to destroy the man's image backfired, and their mistake actually promoted de Gaulle.

In the beginning, Charles de Gaulle had no intention of creating an internal resistance movement within the country. He was under the impression that the army and navy would be able to handle the fight on their own. Then, in front of his eyes, he saw a change in political ethics that would bring down the military's efforts to stop the occupation from happening. But within those occupied regions, he also saw a resistance among its people that was slowly growing. He made it his mission to unite these people and fight for his country's freedom.

Meanwhile...

When the German forces invaded France by the thousands, Jean Rousseau knew that it was time to get out of town. Making the quick decision to pack up their things, along with all of the arrondissement's archives, the Rousseaus moved to the coastal village of Dinard. The village was near St. Malo, and Mr. Rousseau had high hopes that the town would be out of the German's reach and the occupation would not stretch that far. Unfortunately, that is not what the Reich had in mind.

Within weeks of the move, thousands of Nazi soldiers arrived in Dinard. A Hitler-appointed German Field Marshal by the name of Walther von Reichenau moved quickly upon arrival, establishing a base in the center of town. He had been under strict orders to use the base as a headquarters to plan the invasion of Britain. The nervous mayor of Dinard, who was also Rousseau's next-door neighbor, was forced to put in a request for an interpreter to work with the French administration and a liaison to the military commands.

THE FORMATION OF THE FRENCH RESISTANCE

From the moment the French signed the armistice of 1940, there were those who were determined to continue the fight. In a broad sense, the French Resistance was involved in more rebellious activities than they were given credit for. Though the photographs of French Resistance fighters brandishing smuggled British Weapons during the street battles of 1944 hold a particular place in history, the range of activities that resistance members engaged in was all a part of the master plan to, in the words of Churchill, "Set Europe ablaze" (Morris, 2011).

One of the key features of the French Resistance was that it was not a large or powerful organization. Members of the resistance were united by their opposition to the German occupation and their patriotic pride in their country. They did, however, represent a wide variety of political, cultural, and social ideologies. There were trade unionists, veterans of the Spanish Civil War, Republicans who fled Spain, Catholic priests and clergy, doctors, lawyers, and people representing all states of society.

The Urge to Resist

The Allied troops stationed all over the world were forced to decide whether or not to support the Free French or Vichy France. Many units were split in their decision as some elected to join De Gaulle and others chose to support Pétain. In the book *Europe on Trial*, written by Columbia University historian István Deák, the author described how the citizens viewed the split decision throughout the Nazi-occupied regions of France that wished to remain neutral. Deák stated:

For them, both collaboration and resistance were unwelcome, even threatening activities. For many if not most Europeans, the collaborator was a wild-eyed fanatic who tried to get your son to join the Waffen SS … or to work in a German factory, while the resistor was yet another fanatic, likely to be a ragged and unappetizing foreigner who sabotaged train travel and wanted your son to go to the forest and risk being killed there by the Germans. (Deák, 2015)

Within France's borders, the French Army veterans who were able to evade capture had gone underground. The hidden heroes engaged in combat and sabotaged the Germans' operations as the resistance progressed. However, for many people, there was an inciting incident that turned them decisively from passive and submissive to actively resistant. This incident would be the moment the French police and German soldiers started to get overly aggressive as they performed their jobs. The German soldiers were generally kept separate from the French citizens. They tended to stay focused on the main objective of their job, like checking papers and guarding important areas. This being the case, there were still plenty of interactions between the French and the Germans that ranged from friendly and cordial to excessively violent. It was this pervasive German presence that often weighed on the people of France's minds and was always a visible reminder of the massive change that had taken place in only a few short months. As the occupation authorities introduced more invasive restrictions and regulations, many individuals shifted their position from compliant to resistant.

In time, the people of France slowly started to respond to de Gaulle's call to arms, as they began to hide Allied prisoners and soldiers away to keep them safe from the Nazis. They hid Jews where they could not be found, keeping them from being persecuted. Group members made pamphlets about the Nazi regime and passed them out secretly, creating a French Communist party that would become an active participant in the fight against Germany (Evans, 2018). When describing what it meant to be an active member in the Resistance, Deák stated:

To resist meant to leave the legal path and to act as a criminal. In order to be able to print and distribute illegal newspapers, one had to steal strictly controlled printing paper and machines and to forge or steal ration cards, banknotes, residence permits and identity cards. To fight the enemy the resisters needed to seize arms from military garrisons or from rival resisters. All this required the talents of a burglar, a forger and a thief. (Deák, 2015).

These resistance newspapers' earliest appearance was toward the end of 1940 and were usually distributed secretly in the surrounding area. The writers, of course, penned their pieces under pseudonyms, both to protect their identities and give the impression that there were many contributors all writing in opposition to the Germans. German and Vichy authorities began to target these newspapers, but the secret distribution networks made shutting them down entirely a difficult operation. Furthermore, any newspaper that was closed down successfully and its contributors, arrested could be replaced by another network of underground writers and printers. Reading newspapers published by the Resistance became the only source of news about the outside world for the people of France. Otherwise, they were forced to rely on German propaganda for their information. A little light reading became a key act of resistance that people could engage in their day-to-day lives.

Early Resistance Struggles and Limitations

Early on, the Resistance was limited in the number of direct actions it could reasonably take on. These limitations could make an effort to fight the invading forces unsuccessful. The first was the Resistance members' lack of experience when it came to combat training. A vast majority of the French armed forces had been captured and lived in prisoner of war camps established by the Germans, and the French Army under the Vichy regime was held at 10,000 men only. Without the manpower to back them up, how would the Resistance be able to fight?

The second issue related to the same problem the French Army was having, thanks to stipulations agreed on in the armistice. Remember, the Germans had forced the French Army to demobilize their troops. The Germans had also taken a majority of their resources and their weapons. So even if there had been a large number of combat-ready soldiers, the Resistance would still be lacking the materials and arms that they would need to fight. For this reason, their earlier work was limited to primary displays of disobedience and sabotage. Phone lines were cut, some demonstrations were launched, papers and resources were stolen from the occupying forces, and most commonly, underground newspapers began to surface.

All in all, the lack of combat training and resources were things that the Resistance could deal with. The lack of military equipment significantly limited their ability to fight back. Fortunately, this hurdle was soon overcome with Britain's establishment of the Special Operations Executive in July of 1940. This secret organization, informally known as "Churchill's secret army," was established in secret and responsible for defending their country if and when the Nazis invaded (Specktor, 2020). The SOE reached out to all newly-formed resistance groups in France and began providing them with radios, weapons, and perhaps most crucially, instructional training from agents airdropped into France. They smuggled aboard secret planes that landed on hidden airfields in the dead of night. With the support of the SOE and the crucial equipment and support they offered, the Resistance was able to slowly but surely expand its operations beyond the limited reach that they had because of the armistice.

Three years later, in May of 1943, the personal representative of General de Gaulle, Jean Moulin, started the *Conseil National de la Résistance*, or the National Resistance Council. The council proudly stated that they were a federation that would work to join all movements (big or small) in the Resistance. The following year, multiple troops of hostile groups known as *maquis*, or underbrush, derived from the name that the combative soldiers used as cover in the field, combined to form the French Forces of the Interior (FFI). The British SEO organization stayed in regular contact with all of these groups and coordinated all of their activities throughout Europe. The guerilla bands were supported by the Americans, Soviets, and British, while the militias occupied the Axis-controlled territories, providing them with weapons and air-dropping their supplies. The FFI would later take on military operations after the Allies invaded Normandy in support of the Resistance groups and would participate in the uprising that liberated Paris (Britannica, 2021).

Resistance Among the Civilians

Not every form of resistance existed as violent street fighting, assassinations, or sabotage. Resistance existed on a spectrum, and any act of resistance served as an act of defiance against the forces oppressing the civilians. The French civilians found many ways to resist the power of the Nazi soldiers, such as: disregarding minor regulations, refusing to salute, wearing more makeup than the Germans were used to seeing, or speaking French in front of soldiers who could not understand it.

Beyond these subtle slights, there were more active forms of resistance, or at very least displays of distaste towards the Germans. One famous example was the playing of newsreels before films. While there were specific movie theaters reserved solely for the use of Germans, there were also plenty of places Germans and French could watch films together. Before each film, German newsreels would be shown. These short clips were heavily propagandized to reflect the German belief in their absolute victory and often featured speeches of the Führer, Adolf Hitler. In his book *Mein Kampf*, Hitler described how images, such as films, could get people to absorb and understand information more quickly than if they read it. With this belief, he ordered newsreels to be played before each film (Hitler, 1925).

The French cinemagoers were willing to quietly ignore the propaganda at first. However, their patience eventually ran out, and their ability to ignore the information that they were being force-fed turned into heckling, cat-calling, and booing under the cover of the dimly-lit screening room. They would poke fun at Hitler, call the German soldiers on the movie screen vicious names, and make rude remarks about the Germans' predictions of ultimate victory. Determined to put an end to these displays of resistance, the Germans had the cinema lights switched on during the newsreels. The only effect that this had on the movie patrons was that they would simply take their seats after the reels were played.

While acts of opposition like these were hardly going to cripple the Nazi regime, they did show the German soldiers that the population was unwilling to take the occupation lying down. Another form of indirect resistance came in the form of the letter "V". As a show of solidarity with the Allied forces, Belgian refugee Victor de Lavalaye held a BBC broadcast as he requested for the letter to be marked by the French community wherever they could. The letter would serve as a reminder of the Allied's will to victory. Fulfilling the request, the "V" became one of the symbols of the resistance as it was scrawled on pavements, buildings, German vehicles, and as many places that could safely be done. It was not the only symbol of resistance, as the French had their own history and traditions from which to draw, but the "V" did remain a key fixture of visible resistance.

The Double-Edged Sword of War

Just like the resistance that the public was showing, the level of collaboration among the French community varied in many ways. At the same time, the French industry leaders gladly accepted the opportunity to serve along the winning side, and the French police forces willingly enacted anti-Semitic roundups of Jews for deportation. Some simply attempted to carry on their lives by following the rules and regulations imposed by the Germans. The Gestapo relied heavily on French collaborators to lead them and their operations to victory. Anonymous letters would be sent to the occupation authorities accusing people of being members of the Resistance, and many agents would be rounded up and punished on the basis of these letters alone.

Nevertheless, with the help of the SOE, the resistance was able to continue moving forward and able to take a more active role in the war against the Gestapo regime. By 1941, with the German invasion of the Soviet Union, the French Communists were no longer required to engage passively with the Germans. With this, the Resistance gained a number of supporters who were both opposed to the Germans ideologically and their patriotic feelings about France itself. The communists organized strikes to disrupt the German supply lines and actively assassinated German figures. With the armed resistance came German reprisals, often in the form of murdering French civilians at a rate of 50 French for every German killed. These reprisals were seen as a horrendous display of occupational brutality but were also the perfect example of a double-edged sword.

In some cases, they proved to prevent assassinations based on the simple mathematics that a single German was not worth the murder of so many of their own people. Inversely, those within the Resistance felt that cowering to the Nazi's brutality proved that the Germans would be able to brutalize the French into submission. This rift existed throughout the occupation, but one thing was certain: reprisals often acted as a major factor that pushed people into the Resistance.

A GOVERNMENT IN EXILE

The reason behind the sluggish response to de Gaulle's call to arms was the simple fact that the handful of people interested in joining in the fight were based in Britain. However, as the British group began to grow and continue to fight, French volunteers started to travel to the General's London headquarters. The volunteers created an organization that was called Free France, only to change its name in 1941 to the French National Committee. Shortly after the name change, the committee claimed that the legal government of France was in exile.

However, de Gaulle's persistence to be the voice of France struck a few chords. He insisted on being heard and considered a substantial advocate for France's rights in the Allies' council for the next three years. His revoking demands, demeanor, and how he went about it caused a lot of tension from President Franklin Roosevelt and Prime Minister Winston Churchill's side.

As a result of de Gaulle's annoying insistence, President Roosevelt tried his best to sidestep de Gaulle, bringing General Henri Giraud to replace him in 1942. Roosevelt's specific intention to bring Giraud in was so that he could command the liberated French armies that were in North Africa. With that, he could also take over de Gaulle's political role. However, the American President could not have predicted how unsuccessful that plan would work out.

Despite the Allied countries urging him to take a step back, de

Gaulle kept moving forward and went to Algiers in May 1943. He worked his way into Giraud's good graces and became the co-president of a new organization, the French Committee of Liberation. By the end of 1943, he had outmaneuvered and outsmarted Giraud and became the spokesperson for the French resistors.

Resistance Operations

On June 6, 1944, commonly known as D-Day, the Allies truly began to show their support as they invaded Normandy. They had been waiting for their underground supporters to grow large enough to join in on the fight, and it had finally reached that point. The supporters played an important role in the war as they harassed the soldiers and sabotaged the railways and bridges that the Germans needed to cross.

With their pathways in and out of the country destroyed and the persistent harassment of the resistors, the Germans began to fall back. The Resistance organizations counted this as a huge win and started to take their cities back. They took over their local town halls, along with other government buildings, from all Vichy occupiers. Once all of the Vichy officers were expelled from the government buildings and the Resistance had taken over, de Gaulle sent in his own delegates to ensure that the transfer of power ran smoothly.

Paris being liberated was not on top of the Allied force's priority list, and the French Resistance members refused to stand by and wait for them to help. On August 19, 1944, the Resistance forces revolted against the German occupiers in Paris. Lieutenant General Dietrich von Choltitz, the German commander of Paris, was ordered to stop the Resistance's uprising and destroy the entire city. Two weeks earlier, in Warsaw, the same thing had happened when the Polish Home Army tried to push back and seize control. In return, the Germans massacred their city, leaving

7,500 civilians dead, 13,000 wounded, and nearly 90% of their buildings destroyed (Popowycz, 2021).

Now Hitler was ordering Lieutenant General Choltitz to do the same to Paris if there was any sign of an uprising. Charles de Gaulle saw what was happening, and after finding out what happened to the city of Warsaw, he felt the need to interfere. Once he reported the Resistance's uprising to the Allied troops, the Commanding generals sent Major General Jacques-Philippe Leclerc and his Second French Armored Division troops to Paris to infiltrate the city and help with the city's liberation. The first troops arrived in the city in the late hours of August 24, 1944. The next day, American and French soldiers arrived, arresting Choltitz and his men at the Meurice Hotel (LRE Foundation, 2022). The Parisians rejoiced when they heard of the mens' capture and welcomed the American and French soldiers with open arms. The Allied troops took Choltitz and his staff to the Police Department at the edge of Paris, the *Île de la Cité*, and then to the Montparnasse train station. Lieutenant General Choltitz was forced to surrender, and the men were sent on their way.

By October 1944, the United States, British, and Soviet governments had no other choice but to recognize de Gaulle's provisional government and liberation of France. As the sole leader of Free France, de Gaulle and his subordinates were anxious to bring every intelligence group in France into his camp. He wanted to show the American and British governments that all of the groups were working as a united front. De Gaulle would abruptly resign from his position two years later after disagreements with France's political parties as they formed a coalition government (Pickles, 2019).

The Gestapo's Operations to Crush the French Resistance

The Gestapo was not going to back down from the French Resistance without a fight. They still believed they had the upper hand in the war and were willing to up the ante to prove it. They raided homes and businesses, stealing furniture and artwork to send back to Germany. They stripped cities of food and other natural resources, claiming that they were needed to aid the soldiers in the war efforts. They used planes to bombard the railways and streets in an effort to sabotage the resistors' ability to move around. Not to mention that they still had over 2 million of their soldiers and deportees imprisoned in their camps.

In the early years of 1943, the Vichy government formed a paramilitary group to fight the Resistance groups called the *Milice*. This small militia worked as security within the occupied France region and worked closely with the Nazis. The *Milice* members were often more brutal than the Nazistoward Resistance members, often torturing and executing them soon after they were captured.

As stated earlier, any actions that were committed by the Resistance would be met with harsh reprisals. Regarding the punishment for any of the resistor's actions, the Germans policy read, "After each further incident, a number, reflecting the seriousness of the crime, shall be shot" (Herbert, 2004). This policy led to the death of 30,000 Resistance members during France's occupation. On June 10, 1944, the small village of Oradour-sur-Glane saw this policy take place in front of their eyes when the 2nd Waffen-SS Panzer Division invaded their town. The troops swiftly killed 642 of their citizens, looted the homes, and burned the village to the ground (Holocaust Encyclopedia, 2021). What had the small town done so wrong that it equaled the slaughter of nearly their entire population? The Germans had heard a rumor that the city was assisting in the Resistance and was to be made an example of.

Unfortunately for them, not all of the Gestapo's operations paid off. The Resistance began to liquidate the Vichy connections to the country. By the summer of 1944, over 10,000 supporters and Vichy officials were arrested and executed. After dealing with the Vichy supporters, it was the *Miliciens* turn. For their collaboration with the Nazis, an estimated 35,000 *Miliciens* were executed by the French government after the liberation (Jackson, 2003). These executions placed the Gestapo under a great amount of stress, but their stress level was about to get even higher thanks to a certain heroine.

4

LIKE FATHER, LIKE DAUGHTER

Despite being brave and hard-headed like her father, Jeannie remembers their relationship as being slightly strained until her teenage years. He did not speak to her often until she was around the age of thirteen, when he felt that she might have something worthwhile to say. It was then that Jean Rousseau told his teenage daughter about the story of the woman spy that died the year before she was born, Louise de Bettignies. How was he to know that the story of the brave female World War One spy would serve as an inspiration for the impressionable girl in front of him?

EARLIEST SPY WORK

News broke of the mayor's request for a liaison and translator for the German troops. Upon hearing about the request, Jean Rousseau volunteered his daughter, proudly stating that she was fluent in five different languages–one of those languages being German. He told the mayor that "His daughter doesn't want anything but to serve" (Ignatius, 1998).

Jeannie agreed to work as an interpreter for the town's officials, showing up the next morning in her most professional-looking blue suit and white collared shirt. She quickly became the staff favorite among Walter von Reichenau. Her linguistic skills and undeniable beauty quickly caught the eyes of the German soldiers as the delighted men offered her walks on the beach and extravagant gifts. She declined their offers and reiterated what her father told the mayor; she was there to help. However, unbeknownst to the Germans, she was keeping her ears open to what they were saying. She was collecting information and keeping it to herself.

When she was interviewed by *The Washington Post* in 1998, Rousseau recalled how the Germans were still trying to be liked during the time that she was working as an interpreter. She also mentioned how the soldiers were happy that they were able to speak to someone new in their language (Ignatius, 1998). They talked a lot, too. The soldiers told her about names, plans, and numbers. Essentially, everything that they were supposed to keep top-secret. The men talked feverishly as they tried to impress the pretty young girl, not realizing that all of the words that they said were going directly into the vault of her brain.

How the Germans behaved during the first few months after Dinard was occupied was not the only thing that Jeannie remembers. She also recalled what happened one particular night in September of 1940, when a visiting St. Brieuc man learned about Jeannie's job and personally paid her family home a visit. He asked her if she would be willing to share the information that she had overheard or spoken about with the German soldiers. If she were willing to share, he would happily relay that information to the British. Jeannie immediately agreed to tell him all of the secrets and overheard conversations that she had stored in her memory. Rousseau told *The Washington Post* that she remembered telling the man, "What's the point of knowing all that, if not to pass it on?" (Ignatius, 1998). And that is exactly what she did!

A Close Encounter with the Gestapo

Unfortunately for Jeannie, the collection, and subsequent passing, of the learned information made the German soldiers extremely suspicious of her. The British had gained possession of so much intelligence information about what they were doing in the Dinard area that they knew that there had to be a spy leaking information somewhere. The soldiers' suspicions continued to grow until they eventually arrested her in January of 1941. She was taken to a prison in Rennes, where she was interrogated and accused of being a spy. The German army tribunal looked intently at her case, swearing that she had to be a spy. When the officers in Dinard heard about her arrest, they went forward and vouched for her. They swore that she was just a sweet girl willing to translate for them, and there was no possible way that she could be a spy. Due to a lack of evidence, and with the help of the oblivious soldiers who had nothing but nice things to say about her, they were unable to hold her. The Gestapo was forced to release her. However, her release came with a condition. Jeannie Rousseau was ordered to leave the region, forcing her to move to Paris.

Before she left, her father interrogated her himself. He wanted to know what she had done to bring suspicion upon herself and what she said while she was being held at the prison. Jeannie swore that she had not done anything. She was not going to tell her father anything about what she was doing. She was going to tell him the same amount of information that she told the Gestapo during her interrogation–absolutely nothing. Of course, he believed her and never suspected his daughter of anything so dangerous that could put her life in danger. He did not know his daughter as well as he thought.

INTO THE LION'S DEN

She brought an important lesson about spying with her during her move to Paris; listening pays off. When she arrived in the city, she started looking for a job that would help her gain access to sensitive German information. She wanted to find her way back into what she called, "the lion's den" (Olsen, 2019). She was not going to let her close call with the Gestapo slow her down. In fact, it made her want to work even harder and dig deeper than she had before. Jeannie found work as a translator for a syndicate of the national chamber of commerce, The French industrialists. Her solid work ethic paid off just like it had when she worked as the liaison in Dinard. After taking the job, she rose quickly through the ranks and became their top staff member.

Her position allowed her to meet with many important people within the German military, including having regular meetings with the German commanders and their staff at the Hotel Majestic. Her ranking within the organization also required her to discuss commercial issues with the Germans on a daily basis. Jeannie was able to keep tabs on what they were doing and what weapons they had in their possession. She started to feel like all of the information she was gathering did not have a purpose. In Jeannie's own words, "I was storing my nuts, but I had no way to pass them on" (Ignatius, 1998). The opportunity to pass on those stored "nuts" would come when she least expected it.

Chance Encounter or Destiny?

One day, during her regular train commute from Paris to Vichy, Jeannie ran into one of her former classmates from Sciences Po, Georges Lamarque. He was older than she was, 28 or 29, and had a very large build. Jeannie described him as "Not handsome, but had intense searching eyes and a brilliant mind." With no seats available on the train car, they stood in the corridor and took that time to catch up. She told him about the work that she was doing in Paris and how her position gave her consistent contact with the German troops and their high-ranking officials.

Mr. Lamarque told her about his work with a network called Alliance, led by Madame Marie-Madeleine Fourcade. Although the group's official name was Alliance, the Gestapo had a nickname for them. With the agents of the Alliance using animal and bird names as their alias, the Axis forces found it amusing to call them Noah's Ark. Lamarque, whose alias was Petrel, had been given the task of organizing a small subset outfit called Druids, in order to gather information on the Germans.

The main group, the Alliance, had a simple goal: supply the American and British commanding officers with the most vital German military secrets that they could get their hands on. This would include sailing schedules for the submarines, troop movements, coastal fortifications, and gun emplacements. The espionage group had grown significantly by the time Jeannie was invited to join, estimated at about 3,000 agents. Not only was the size of the group impressive, but they all held different positions within society. There were lawyers, priests, plumbers, students, housewives, architects, and actors, just to name a few. Despite the different occupations, Madame Fourcade made sure of one thing: that the group would include the highest number of female agents of any organization in the Resistance. She was successful in this feat, with almost 20% of her recruits being women.

The subnetwork was to be headed by Lamarque, and he was solely responsible for recruiting his own agents and all of the administration work. The Druids' name came from the pre-Christian Celtic priesthood of the British Isles. The group proved to be considerably valuable early on, especially after a mass arrest of Gestapo members at the beginning of 1943. Many of the arrested German soldiers were responsible for attacking large cities in southern France. Fourcade pushed Lamarque to recruit new leaders for the Alliance sectors and send them to rebuild the invaded areas. In June of 1943, Lamarque was sent to London for more advanced training by the M16 troops. That was when he ran into his old friend, Jeannie.

Knowing about her previous work as an interpreter in Dinard, as well as her close encounter with the German soldiers, Georges thought that Rousseau would be a great addition to the group. She was to be known under the code name, Amniarix. Jeannie did not hesitate for a second, eagerly accepting his offer immediately. The two got to work right away as Rousseau began to divulge all of the information that she had been keeping in her memory. When Jeannie looked back at the time that she unfolded all of this gathered intelligence to Georges, she said, "I used my memory. I knew all the details about the plants and commodities in Germany. We were building up knowledge of what they had, what they did; we could keep an eye on what they were doing—we' being me. And I couldn't be dangerous, could I?" (Ignatius, 1998).

The two started to make plans for their own type of attack, an attack using her intelligence. She told Georges about how certain offices inside the Hotel Majestic were out of bounds for everyone besides German soldiers. Those were where they worked on plans for secret projects and special weapons. Even though they were out of bounds, Jeannie was sure that she could manage to infiltrate the restricted areas. That day came when some of the soldiers that she became friends with in Denard were sent to Paris to work in a different office than she normally visited. These soldiers were the same men that vouched for her, insisting that she was merely a charming girl working as a translator. They were still under the assumption that this sweet girl could do no wrong and introduced her to their friends.

Delighted to see their old friend from Dinard, the German soldiers offered to take her out for drinks that evening. After a few drinks, they started to drop subtle hints that they were there to work on some top-secret projects that involved weapons of war. Completely enamored by the intelligent young woman, Jeannie's old friends introduced her to new ones. These new friends were high-ranking officials that would also grow close to her as time went on. By staying close to these men, Jeannie Rousseau had crushed her first goal. She had gotten into the Lion's Den, and that den was packed with useful details that would help the British defeat the Germans. All she had to do was keep her mouth closed and her ears open; the information would come to her.

5

THE GERMAN ROCKET PROGRAMME

As the war dragged on and Germany's luck began to reverse, Allied bombing raids began to target German cities with devastating results. With the *Luftwaffe*, the German airforce, incapable of launching any further attacks on Britain due to losses sustained throughout the preceding years, the secret development of unmanned flying bombs and rocket munitions was ramped up. Theoretical development had begun as early as 1940, but in 1943 production on the so-called *Vergeltungswaffen*, the "Vengeance Weapons" or "V-weapons," began to ramp up.

NAZI WONDER WEAPONS

German weapon designers had a long history of wild and impressive experiments when it came to producing unconventional weapons. During the First World War, the impressive Paris Gun, designed by Fritz Rausenberger, had an effective range of 130 kilometers and was used to bombard Paris from 120 kilometers away in Northern France. The distance the gun could fire from was so incomprehensible that it was initially believed that the attack resulted from a high-altitude zeppelin bombing raid. In any case, although casualties were relatively low, the psychological effect of the weapon saw thousands of Parisians attempt to flee the city in the days and weeks following its use.

At the end of the war, the Paris gun was dismantled. The reason for its destruction was that it was one of the conditions of the Treaty of Versailles. However, the concept of creating super-weapons remained at the forefront of Hitler's mind as he started planning Germany's revenge on the Allied forces. By 1942, the Reich was focusing more on the development of these weapons than the spread of their propaganda. They hoped that the weapons would make the war change course in their direction. These weapons ranged from tanks and self-propelled guns to jet aircraft and assault rifles. In some cases, they sped up the weapons' development so that they could be used on the battlefield.

Due to the Treaty of Versailles, the German army was prohibited from owning or using tanks during World War 1. Once Hitler came into power in 1933, he began to slowly rebuild his tank force. This secret rebuild began with a series of *Panzerkampfwagen* tanks, or Panzer for short—the tanks that they planned on using during World War II, the Pz. IV were plated with thicker steel armor, mounted with two machine guns and a 75-mm gun, could reach speeds up to 25 miles per hour, and had exceptional mobility. As the war continued, they rolled out the next version to aid the Pz. IV. This version was called the Pz. V, or the Panther. The Panther could reach a top speed of 28 miles per hour, and a slope was added to the rear, causing shells to ricochet off of the back (Britannica, 2020).

The StG 44 rifle, or what Hitler called the "Storm Gun," was deployed from 1943 on and allowed soldiers to match the rate of fire of their enemies. The Germans also released two smaller firearms during the war: the MP series of folding stock machine guns and the 98k bolt action carbine. The StG 44 rifle had many advantages, like the ability to quickly and easily strip it down in the field, hold 30 rounds in its magazine, and be controllable when used under automatic fire. However, the bullet rounds used less gunpowder and went a short distance, thus making the impact less lethal (Mizokami, 2018).

For the German air force, jet fighters like the Me-262, or *Messer-schmitt* Schwalbe, suffered similar fates. The Me-262 could fly considerably faster than most conventional airplanes, with its speed ranging from 460 to 540 miles per hour. It had four 30-mm cannons attached and carried 1,000 pounds of bombs. The jet's advanced design was difficult to mass-produce, with only 300 out of the 1,400 made ever seeing combat. The Germans also lacked the fuel and spare parts to keep up with the maintenance. Many of the jets were not able to make it to full production due to the destruction of Germany's transportation system, causing interference in the import of needed parts. The limited number in production and resources made the jets, not the ultimate war-winning tool they were supposed to be, making less of an impact on the war than they could have. Again, Nazi jet fighters performed admirably when they were deployed, but they offered little strategic gain simply for the fact that there was no way to produce more of them or pilots that were trailed well enough to make a difference (NMAF, 2022).

The *Schwere Gustav*, or "Hitler's giant gun," a railway gun that entered service in 1941, was the largest caliber gun ever fired in combat. This 800-mm caliber gun weighed over 1,350 tons and was capable of launching a 4.8 metric ton projectile over 47 kilometers away with a velocity of 820 meters per second. The idea for the gun was conceived before the beginning of World War II, and Hitler demanded that it be built before the invasion of France. Designed with the sole intention of cracking the defensive forts on the Maginot Line, the Schwere Gustav had to be able to penetrate one meter of steel plating or 7 meters of reinforced concrete.

Despite the weapon being classified as a railway gun, its large size made it restrictive in mobility. In fact, the gun had to be transported in pieces and assembled at the site.

The enormous gun took weeks to deploy, needed a crew of 500 to operate it, and required a whole section of railway laid down for it to fire from. The large weapons production took too long to produce and missed out on the invasion of France, but would see other combat action. Missing out on the breaking of the Maginot Line, it was transported to the East coast and played a big part in Operation Barbarossa. The gun's overall value to the war was somewhat limited. It cost an exceptional amount of money and energy to design, develop, and produce. Considering the lengthy setup and breakdown processes, along with the fact that it took 45 minutes to reload, the gun was easy to target from the air before it could be effectively deployed.

While the Schwere Gustav at least made it to the front lines when it was deployed, most of the *Wunderwaffe*, or "Wonder Weapons", proved to be little more of an ill-conceived resource that the Nazi economy could not support the development or production of. While often extraordinary and instructive for future arms development, the *Wunderwaffe* program was ultimately doomed to fail by Germany's strategic and economic position just as their need for such weapons became more crucial. In most cases, the rate of development, effectiveness, and a number of these wonder weapons were greatly exaggerated. With many of them, particularly the Panzer tank, the Germans were more focused on getting the weapons to their soldiers than whether they were working properly. Nevertheless, the weapons mentioned above served their purpose considerably well over the course of the war. Hitler knew that if he wanted to make a lasting impression on the Allied troops and win the war, he would have to come up with something better–something that caused more destruction.

HITLER HAS LIFT-OFF

On October 3, 1942, a group of German engineers and scientists watched the launchpad from the assembly building in Peenemünde. On that launchpad stood a five-story tall black-and-white rocket. As the men watched the rocket intensely, vapor clouds started to build, a loud siren let out a wail, and the numbers on the countdown dropped lower. When the countdown hit zero, the rocket shot out flames from the bottom and rose through the air with a loud roar.

It began to rise from the launchpad, and within seconds, the rocket was in the stratosphere. It quickly broke the sound barrier and headed east, exactly as planned. The rocket traveled a distance of 120 miles before it crashed just short of the Baltic coast. The director of the Peenemünde testing site, Luftwaffe General Walter Dornberg, was overjoyed when he heard the news. The first test flight of the V-2 rocket was a success. His team had created the world's first long-range missile. With the successful testing of the rocket, Dornberg told the V-2 project director, Wernher von Braun, that "The new superweapon must be put into production as soon as possible for the Führer and victory" (Olson, 2019).

Peenemünde was once a tiny village in northern Berlin before the German soldiers took it over in 1936. They tore down the homes and buildings, replacing them with a missile testing and launching site–making sure that the site would be the largest in the world's history. Along with Germany's top engineers and scientists, Von Braun, worked together at the site to create the newest aerial weapons. The type of aerial weapons that the world had never seen or thought of before, more specifically the long-range rocket, called the V-2, and the pilotless jet that was armed with bombed, called the V-1. The V-1 rockets were commonly known as "buzz bombs," due to the buzzing sound that you heard before they landed. This buzzing sound would make them an easy target to be shot down, which is why the V-2 bombs came in handy. The V-2s were completely silent until the moment of impact. Weapons on these would wreak havoc on his enemies, which is good because the Germans were barely hanging on as the Resistance operations grew stronger, fighting the Occupiers any chance they could.

The V-2's success came at a critical time for Hitler and his soldiers. They were soon to face two major defeats on the battlefield, in North Africa and Stalingrad, and the success of these aerial weapons was sure to help them regain some momentum. Their mass production became Hitler's number one priority in the early months of 1943, as he assigned thousands of the prisoners in their labor camps to build them and poured large amounts of money into the cause. The Führer told his war generals that the new weapons would turn the war in their favor and predicted that London would be leveled by the end of 1943. Once London was destroyed, Britain would have no choice but to surrender. The V-2 rockets were scheduled to launch for the first attack on October 20, 1943 (Olsen, 2019).

THE FRENCH RESISTANCE VS. THE ROCKET SITES

During the time of the V-weapons development, nearly 9,000 Resistance members were held and used for slave labor in the icy underground tunnels. The working conditions were deplorable and unsafe, injuring and becoming the cause of death of many workers. Within the first eight months of being sent to the Mittelbau-Dora concentration camp in Nordhausen, over 4,500 French deportees died. The weather was too cold for the back-breaking work that they were forced to perform, and the underground constraints deprived them of fresh air and sunlight.

Besides the cold weather, the slave laborers worked eighteen hours a day and returned to their lice-infested bunks to go to sleep.

The act of starvation, mixed with their bad hygiene, caused a rise in diarrhea and typhoid fever. If that was not enough, the prisoners were often beaten or killed by the guards if they could not keep up with the others. Amongst the deportees, there was a small amount of prejudice. French and Belgian Resistance members were considered more valuable than the others. They were often given better jobs, including performing more of the skilled work on the rockets.

Despite the depraved conditions of the labor camp and the tightened security, the Resistance members still found any opportunity to fight back. Information slowly began to trickle through the cracks, finding its way back to British intelligence. The British government was not oblivious to the fact that the Germans were building guided bombs along the Atlantic coast; they simply lacked the details of the specific locations and what type of missiles they were testing.

The Germans felt that the Resistance was getting information in some way and started to make changes to how things were run. In April of 1944, they started to bring in new workers from other labor camps, most of them being Yugoslavs, Russians, and Ukrainians. These new laborers replaced many of the French workers as a way for the Nazis to prevent any information from being leaked from the camp to the Resistance. Too bad they could not stop their own soldiers from spreading their secrets after a few drinks. The happy drunks were willingly giving the information away to a sweet girl named Madeleine Chauffour, hoping to impress her.

6

ROUSSEAU SPIES ON THE
ROCKETS

Working with Georges Lamarque and his Druids espionage outfit in Paris, Jeannie Rousseau got down to business. Going under the guise of a woman named Madame Madeleine Chauffour, she turned on the charm and started to get close to the Nazi soldiers using her cunning nature. She would taunt and tease them, thinking that they had a chance with her in order to coax vital information out of them.

Rousseau's attractive looks, intelligence, and fluency in German obtained many invitations to the soldiers' drinking parties at a house on the Avenue Hoche. Once the drinks started flowing, the bragging would begin and Jeannie was right there to listen in on what they were saying. They spoke freely about their work, and would frequently talk to her about a base on Germany's Baltic coast where soldiers were creating secret weapons.

Jeannie insists that she never played into the spy game known as "Mata Hari," or sold sex for secrets. Instead, she would use her wits to charm the plans out of the soldiers and her ears to listen to every minuscule detail. Remembering the events of those parties that were held near the Arc de Triomphe, she told a journalist, "I had become part of the equipment, a piece of furniture. I was such a little one, sitting with them, and I could not but hear what was said. And what they did not say, I prompted." (Olson 2019). The German soldiers would get drunk and start to talk to her, believing that Madeleine Chauffour was merely a naive German girl. Jeannie remembers how she would stand there wide-eyed in belief as they bragged about the military's plans in such incredible detail, only to pass the divulged information onto Lamarque later on.

An Eager Guard Accidently Helps the Cause

One German soldier made Jeannie's job easier for her. During one of the many drinking parties that the soldiers were holding, the men spoke about Germany's new weapon that could fly long distances and was faster than an airplane. Rousseau, still playing her part as the young, naive girl, told the soldiers that they must be mad. She recalls repeatedly telling them, "What you are telling me cannot be true!" (Ignatius, 1998). In many ways, she was shocked about the details regarding the new top-secret weapons, but she was more surprised that they were handing the information over willingly. All it cost her was her time and a few mugs of beer!

An overeager guard, determined to show her that he was telling her the truth and annoyed with her level of skepticism, offered to show her the plans. He pulled out a piece of paper with the plans on them and revealed them to her. That particular piece of paper held all of the information that Jeannie had been searching for. The paper showed the Germans' plans to build V-1 and V-2 rockets that were being developed by Colonel Max Wachtel's team at a testing plant in Peenemünde. It also contained a drawing of the rockets, where the sites were, where to enter the sites, and what specific color passes one would need to enter certain areas.

After she left the party, Rousseau drove straight to the Druids' safe house that was located on the Left Bank. Once she arrived, she wrote down everything that she heard and everything that she saw. Her incredible photographic memory allowed her to remember everything word for word, she did not need to paraphrase, and she was not required to understand what they were talking about. Luckily, there were people who did have a great level of understanding about what the soldiers were speaking about because Jeannie did not have a clue about most of it. She knew was that whatever they were talking about in their drunken state was very serious, and she suspected that it might be one of Germany's biggest secrets in their effort to win the war.

The drawings did not make any sense to Jeannie when she looked at them, but thanks to her photographic memory, she was able to describe the plans in extraordinary detail to Lamarque.

After a few months of these gatherings and subsequent purging of the information to Georges, a detailed report was ready to be sent off to England. On top of the prepared report, he included a forward regarding the information, "This material looks preposterous. But I have total faith in my source" (Ignatius, 1998). Jeannie was not sure if the high-ranking British officials would ever receive her report, and if they did receive it, would the information be of any use to them. She recalled that during that waiting period, she felt "the chilling fear, the unending waiting, the frustration of not knowing whether the dangerously obtained information would be passed on–or passed on in time" (Olsen, 2019).

However, there was no need to worry. Georges had successfully passed on the information to Madame Marie-Madeleine Fourcade, who then sent it on to the next level of the intelligence group. When Madame Fourcade first received Rousseau's report, she was extremely impressed. It was easily the best report that she had read in the past two years, full of the details that other spies had been striving to get. She asked Georges who his source was, to which he answered Amniarix. Lamarque refused to give away the spy's real name, only telling Fourcade that his source was a "gifted linguist" and all of the information in the report had been acquired firsthand (Olson, 2019).

The detailed plans, now known as the "Wachtel's Report," would then be passed down to military intelligence expert and Oxford physicist, Reginald Jones. He then passed it on until it reached Prime Minister Winston Churchill, finally giving him the final bit of information that he needed in order to bomb the site. As the report revealed, Churchill saw what he feared most, "that the final stage has been reached in developing a stratospheric bomb of an entirely new type" (Mundy, 2017). In September of 1943, plans were being made by the British to deploy 500 bombers to the Peenemünde facility, hoping to derail the Nazi's plans and save thousands of innocent people.

Jeannie's report, giving significant detail about all of the information that she had learned, would later become considered one of the most important documents in World War II history. An excerpt of this amazing piece of history read:

It appears that the final stage has been reached in developing a stratospheric bomb of an entirely new type. This bomb is reported to be 10 cubic meters in volume and filled with explosives. It would be launched almost vertically to reach the stratosphere as quickly as possible . . . initial velocity being maintained by successive explosions. . . . The trials are understood to have given immediate excellent results as regards accuracy and it was to the success of these trials that Hitler was referring when he spoke of new weapons that will change the face of the war when the Germans use them. . . .A German officer estimates that 50-100 of these bombs would suffice to destroy London. The batteries will be sited so that they can methodically destroy most of Britain's large cities during the winter. (Jones, 1978)

7

THE RAID ON PEENEMÜNDE

On August 17, 1943, all of the information that Jeannie Rousseau had provided to the British Intelligence networks was put to good use. British group commanders received a preliminary report from the Bomber Command headquarters, relaying a message that the raid on Peenemünde would be taking place that night. The briefing that would be held at the headquarters was highly secured as the group commanders were given orders on how Operation Hydra would be handled and carried out. Prime Minister Churchill told his men that the Peenemünde site was being used to develop superweapons and it would need to be attacked "on the heaviest possible scale" (Holmey, 2021).

OPERATION HYDRA

'Operation Hydra' has three important requirements and a specific list of objectives that would need to be fulfilled if it were to be successful. The requirements were that the moon needed to be full or nearly full, the targeted site needed to be cloud-free, and the weather over Britain needed to be clear to ensure the bomber's safe return. As a means of diversion, some of the Mosquito aircraft would be sent to raid Berlin. This diversionary tactic would be known as 'Operation Whitetail'. During the briefing, crews were made well aware that they would need to make a return flight home the next night if they had not of inflicted enough damage on the targeted site.

The objectives of the attack were crystal clear. They needed to kill as many personnel as possible who were responsible and involved in the research and development of the V-weapons. In order to do that, they would need to bomb the worker's quarters. They would also need to render the research facilities useless while destroying as much research, documents, and V-weapons as possible.

The flyers had a long flight ahead of them as they crossed over the North Sea, flew through the narrow opening of Jutland, and crossed over Zeeland and Funen. After they crossed the Baltic, they would be able to approach the targeted site on the Arkona Peninsula. Most of the bombers made it to the Peenemünde testing site with little to no interference, while the rest of them were headed to Berlin for the diversionary raid. Berlin was chosen because the Germans believed that if they were to get attacked, that would be the location where the bombing would begin. The raid on Peenemünde would truly be unexpected.

The Raid

It was almost midnight when von Braun got back to his room, ready for bed after a night of partying with his colleagues at the officers' club. It was a beautiful, clear night, and some of the officers were still outside as they enjoyed the festivities. Wernher was just about to fall asleep when a loud air siren started to go off. They were under attack, and he was not even dressed. He threw on some clothes and got on the testing site's communications line to get a status report telling him what was going on. He was told that there were multiple waves of bombers, believed to be English, that were over Denmark. It was also believed that they were headed to Berlin, not Peenemünde.

The attacks came in three waves, all well-synchronized and timed out to the second. The bombers flew at an abnormally low height, about 6,000 feet above the ground. At 00:11 military time, the first wave of airmen flew over the target, calling in new Pathfinders and directing the crew where to bomb. They shot out white tracers, red markers, and a fogging system that signaled to the next wave where to bomb. After the markers were dropped, the German soldiers loaded up their anti-aircraft guns and started shooting into the sky.

Von Braun and some of his men ran to the air raid bunker; but by the time they arrived, the first round of bombs was already being dropped. At 00:31, Ninety 4,000-bombs and 7,000 1,000-pound bombs were dropped on the rocket storage facility. The bombs decimated the facility and the V2s that were inside. At 00:43, the third wave dropped bombs on the Peenemünde site's laboratory, destroying all of the German scientist's data, research, and scientific equipment. Within minutes, almost six hundred British frontline air units had swept the island and dropped fire-causing and highly explosive bombs.

Due to the close distance, the airmen could vividly recall what they saw that night, from the spotlights and tracers to the explosions on the ground and in the air. One airman remembered how the fires from the explosion and chemicals looked like a firework display. On the return trip to England, the flyers were told that the raid they had just completed would greatly impact the war.

THE IMPACT OF OPERATION HYDRA ON THE WAR

The Raid was a success, or so the Allied troops thought. They had destroyed the facility, including the living quarters, technical workshops, production plant, and laboratory. A majority of the models and blueprints for the V-2 weapons had been destroyed, and most of the key equipment needed to build the rockets was damaged beyond repair. They had managed to kill 180 researchers and German soldiers. However, in a strange twist of irony, they had accidentally killed 170 enslaved laborers when they bombed the labor camp in error. Some of the laborers were the same Resistance members that had passed on information about the weapons in the first place. Most of the bombers made it back home safely, but some were not so lucky. German night-fighters were hot on their tail, shooting down and killing 40 airmen.

Back at the testing site, a dazed and confused Wernher von Braun opened the door of the bomb shelter to find the testing site in complete ruins. One of the Peenemünde workers could only describe the burning facility as "a veritable sea of flames" (Olsen, 2019). Von Braun rushed into his burning office, attempting to save any plans documents that were still salvageable. He was able to find a few papers before he was forced out by the hot flames and smoldering smoke.

Despite the damage that the bombing caused, Hitler still had plans to go forward. After the raid, the workers were forced to leave the Peenemünde testing site and all research was put on hold for several months. Unfortunately for the German officials, the halting of the production and research affected their main goal of interfering with the Allied invasion of France in June of 1944.

The V-2 was initially designed to be used at the same time as the V-1. However, due to the raid and issues with production, the Germans would have to postpone using the missile. Hitler decided to go ahead with his plan eight months after the originally planned launching date, and one week after D-Day, when the V-1 missile was finally launched at Britain on June 13, 1944 (Olsen, 2019). For the next three months, thousands of the German's pilotless missiles rained down on the city of London. The death toll skyrocketed, killing more than 6,000 of its citizens and injuring almost 16,000. The homes within the London limits, and its bordering cities, were estimated at nearly 23,000 houses that were irreparable. Although the lives of citizens were lost and family homes were demolished, the V-1s alone caused considerably less damage than if both missiles had been launched. The smallest of silver linings with the bombings was that out of the 8,500 rockets that were launched, only a third of them reached their target. If all of the missiles had reached their destination, the death toll and damage that occurred would have been much worse.

Having known about the bombs in advance, London had time to counteract the attacks. They worked on their plans when it came to their anti-aircraft defenses, hoping that they could lower the impact of when they were eventually launched. The showering of V-1 missiles came to an abrupt end in September of 1944, when the Allied forces overran the France launching sites. The residents of the country were relieved, but that relief was short-lived. On the eighth of September, Hilter ordered his generals to launch the V-2 rockets (Olsen, 2019). The residents of London were much more terrified of this rocket than the missile, as it caused a small earthquake every time one struck the ground. The rocket traveled faster than the speed of sound, and no one could hear it coming–until it hit its target. The British capital was peppered with these rockets, finally ending a few short months before the war was over. The death toll, in the end, was much lower than with the V-1s, this time killing almost 3,000 people.

If the production and testing of the V-2s had not been delayed by the raid on Peenemünde, the rockets would have been fired months earlier. Without the months of postponement, London would have suffered much more damage and lost thousands more innocent lives. When asked about the raid's impact on the German Rocket Programme, Winston Churchill replied, "Although we could do little against the rocket once it was launched, we postponed and substantially reduced the weight of the onslaught" (Olsen, 2019). Sadly, Jeannie Rousseau did not get to see how her information had helped save these lives. She was busy trying to save her own.

8

A HARROWING ESCAPE

After the raid, Jeannie continued to dive deeper into her work and reported the information back to England. Her continued employment with the French Industrialists made her job much easier. She would travel deep into Germany with them and report the things that she heard and saw first-hand when she returned. She would give Lamarque the technical details about the rockets, even though she did not understand them. He would then pass them down the line to be sent off to Prime Minister Churchill.

Churchill and his high-ranking officials were blown away by the amount of detail Jeannie was providing in her reports. They requested for her to come to London for a debriefing. They preferred for her to come in the Spring of 1944, but the weather and unclear night skies made it impossible for her to be picked up by plane. Instead, they arranged for her to come by sea a few days before what would be known as D-Day.

She and two other spies, Robert Douin and Jacques Stosskopf, fled to Treguier with the intention of meeting up with a fellow Druid contact. Their contact's job was to guide them through the minefields so they could climb aboard a boat waiting for them.

Unfortunately, Rousseau and her fellow agents did not receive word that their contact's cover had been blown and had been arrested the night before. The agent would not be there to help them when they arrived.

Their contact may not have been waiting for them when they arrived, but the German police were. The house where they were supposed to meet their contact at was surrounded by soldiers. Jeannie had arrived at the house first and saw the officers waiting for them. She tried to warn her fellow agents that they were walking into a trap, but it was too late. The three agents were arrested the moment that they were spotted. Rousseau tried her best to save the two other agents, distracting the German soldiers by screaming in their native tongue. Her distraction tipped off one of the agents to make a run for it; however, the other agent did not follow suit. Terrified of the German soldiers' reprisals on his hometown of Treguier, the agent had refused to flee.

AMNIARIX: FROM SPY TO PRISONER

The soldiers took Jeannie, and their other captured Druid agent to Rennes to be interrogated. She knew what to expect from the interrogation. After all, it was the same prison where she had been taken in 1940 the first time she was interrogated. While she was being questioned, she gave the Gestapo her papers that showed her name as "Madeline Chauffeur". The soldiers did not connect the alias with the name of the girl that they had interrogated years ago when they had suspected the charming young girl of being a spy.

When asked why she was traveling to London, Jeannie showed the soldiers the two dozen pairs of nylon stockings in her bag. She had planned to give the nylon stockings to her handlers when she reached London to thank them for their work. However, in the interrogation room, she used the items to her advantage. She told the soldiers that she was selling the stockings on the black market. Jeannie was happy that the men were so oblivious and believed her story. If they had not believed her or worked harder to connect her alias to her real name, the events that followed would have turned out much worse for her. Call it luck that the Gestapo's interrogator did not look harder into her life and realize her true identity. His negligence would be the determining factor that ended up saving her life and kept the guards flustered at her next stop. Jeannie was to be sent to a labor camp, while the other two agents that had been traveling with her were to be executed.

Ravensbruck

Jeannie's story quickly went from a spy story to a survival story when she arrived at Ravensbruck. She told a journalist, "Once you were caught, you did not think about what you were fighting for anymore. You thought only of surviving. You were beaten. You were desperate. You were incapable of thinking of the future. You thought of one thing—yourself, and of surviving" (Ignatius, 1998). She arrived at the women's concentration camp on August 15, 1944. The dossier that contained the name "Madame Chauffeur" and her work with the espionage ring had been sent separately and hadn't arrived yet. When the guards demanded that she tell them her name, she told them her real name. The guards took her for her word and somehow never managed to connect the two names together. If they had, the Nazis would have realized that they had a spy in their midst.

The women within the camp were in extremely bad health, many of them barely alive by the time Jeannie arrived. Some of the prisoners had been there for a year, many of them longer. Besides their disintegrating health, Rousseau could tell that their hope to be saved was depleting as well. As a new arrival at the camp, she took it upon herself and made it her duty to lift those hopes. She told them about D-Day, telling the women, "The Allies had landed. They are behind us. They are coming" (Ignatius, 1998).

Rousseau had a special connection with two French Resistance workers who arrived at the camp with her, Marinette Curateau and Germaine de Renty. Curateau was a communist Montmartre, and Renty was a countess that had been involved in multiple resistance operations. The three strong-willed women came together to make a pact, they would not help build the Nazi's war machine, and they would protest if they were sent to a work camp. No matter how dangerous their protest would be, they refused to support any efforts that would help the Germans win the war.

Torgua and Königsberg

Shortly afterward, she was sent, along with 500 other prisoners, to the Torgau facility in Saxony. The camp was attached to an explosive and firearm factory, where she and the other women were being forced to build guns and weapons for the German soldiers. The conditions at the camp were much better than in Ravensbruck; however, Jeannie stayed true to her and her friend's pact. She would not stand for it and used her brilliance to keep all of the women from helping the Germans as they fought the Allied troops. Once they arrived at the facility, Rousseau approached the camp commander. She told him, in perfect German, that under the Geneva Convention, she and her fellow Frenchwomen prisoners were forbidden from producing firearms for them. Her defiance raised the women's spirits, and they too refused to make ammunition.

The commander ordered the women to stand down or face being sent back to Ravensbruck. Some of the women preferred staying at *Torgau* and did not want to be sent back to Ravensbruck, but Rousseau urged them to hold their positions. Later she stated, "You see, I was convinced somebody had to do something. Some-

74

body had to stand up. I decided to do it" (Sebba, 2017). Not all of the women were appreciative of the stand that Jeannie took at the ammunition factory. Loulou Le Porz, a fellow prisoner at the Torgau camp, thought that the small protest that Jeannie started amongst the women showed terrible judgment. "She was unusual, impulsive. Of course, it is all very well to have courage, but you must know how to use it" (Holmey, 2021).

The scene did not come without consequences. After her small protest, she was sent back to Ravensbruck for another round of questioning. Once again, she confused the guards at the camp by giving her real name. The guards had a hard time searching for papers that contained the name "Jeannie Rousseau" because they did not exist. The guards would then ask her why she was there, and she would tell them that she did not know.

The camp officials had no idea who this woman was, and concluded that this woman was a troublemaker. Due to Rousseau's actions at the factory and spreading the news of D-Day among the women, their hopes were now high, and they believed that liberation would be coming soon. With the heightened sense of hope, they would soon start to protest the German efforts to make them work. The guards placed the small uprising all on Jeannie. Their frustration with her caused them to send her to Königsberg for punishment, with or without papers. Rousseau remembers the camp as being "a very bad place" (Ignatius, 1998).

The women prisoners were forced to work outside in the freezing cold, hauling gravel and large rocks to build an airstrip for the German planes. At night they would be allowed to come out of the blistering cold weather and were given one bowl of hot soup. The soup was held in large vats and was monitored by the head guard, a large woman she came to know as "La Vachere". Jeannie recalled how vile and cruel the woman was to the prisoners, often kicking over the vat of hot soup into the snow and laughing as she watched the starving women scramble to eat the slushy meal.

However, the cruelty of La Vachere and the other guards did not stop Jeannie from fighting. She got it in her head that if people outside the prison knew that they were there, that they were alive, it would increase the probability of more prisoners surviving. Jeannie started gathering the women's names and built a census that included the names of 400 women being housed inside those fences. She would write the name on a small piece of paper and drop them through the fence where they would be collected by French prisoners of war that were being held in a camp nearby. She was not sure what would happen with the names after that point, but she had to do something. Somehow, the French POWs managed to take all of those small pieces of paper, put them together on a list, and get the list to the Red Cross in Switzerland.

Jeannie's health was starting to deteriorate, and the escalating punishment that she received from the guards only made it worse. From the winter of 1944 to 1945, the women started off each morning by stripping down naked and being sprayed with a hose. They were then instructed to stand there in the bitter cold until the water froze before they were allowed to go back inside. With her health getting worse by the day, Jeannie realized that if she did not figure out a way to escape Königsberg, then she was going to die.

The day came when she was able to come up with a plan to escape, a bizarre plan that could get her killed, but a plan no less. After some of the women contracted typhoid, a truck was set up to transport the sick prisoners to the gas chambers back in Ravensbruck. Jeannie got the message about the dangerous transport to her two French friends whom she arrived at the camp. The three women hid in the truck packed with prisoners and endured the two-day journey without any food.

Once the truck reached the gates of Ravensbruck, it was time to complete the rest of their plan. The truck was required to wait inside the gates for a few minutes before it headed to the gas chambers and the three women took that time to sneak out of the truck and back into the camp. They were hoping that they could creep into the camp while the guards were not looking, and then infiltrate a group of other prisoners without being noticed.

Back to Ravensbruck

Once they filtered into the prison camp, they rushed back to where the French prisoners were held, in Barrack 22. They knew that they would need their fellow prisoners' help desperately if they were going to stay alive. Since they had snuck back in, they no longer had an assigned prison number. Without an assigned prison number, they would have no access to shelter or food. After telling the women their harrowing escape story, the ladies agreed to take them in for one night only. The next night, Jeannie and her three friends were stealthily moved over to the Polish barracks, which housed and fed them for a few days. They could have stayed in the barracks longer if one of the prison informants had not told the authorities about her and her friends' escape from Königsberg.

The guards did not take kindly to Rousseau and the two other prisoners making them look incompetent, and sent them to another prison inside the facility. All three of the women were interrogated and beaten for hours. When Jeannie was asked how they managed to get released from the interrogation, she told a journalist, "The three of us told 10 different stories. I myself told two or three" (Ignatius, 1998). They made her pay for her shenanigans, only feeding her portions and ordering her to complete the dirtiest jobs in the facility. Her health was wavering, and the dirty jobs, like cleaning the latrines, only made her feel worse.

A NEGOTIATED RELEASE

Eventually, all of Jeannie's hard work to create a census of the women prisoners paid off. The Swiss Red Cross arrived at the gates of Ravensbruck and read off a list of names of women that were to be released, the list that Jeannie had created. She listened intently inside of her barracks, waiting for her name to be called. When she finally heard it, she started to rush toward the door, making her way toward freedom. But the guards were not going to let her go that easily. One man stepped in front of the door, blocking her escape, and informed her that she would not be receiving a humanitarian release. She knew that if she stayed at Ravensbruck any longer, she was going to die there. The only thing that kept her going was the hope that the Red Cross would return.

Her wish came true when the Swiss Red Cross arrived at the camp's gates a few days later with another list of names. Jeannie suspected that her name would be on the list again since she had not left with them the last time. Despite her sickness and threat of physical harm, she mustered up the nerve to start screaming at the Nazi soldier that was holding her. Jeannie started to intimidate the guard, telling her, "You will be in terrible trouble after the war ends. They know I'm here. They will come after you and find you, and punish you" (Ignatius, 1998).

The words from the half-dead woman did their job, leaving her shaken. The frightened guard allowed Jeannie, Marinette, and Germaine to leave the barrack and board the Red Cross bus. Jeannie felt like she was waking up from a terrible nightmare as they drove away from the camp and drove toward the Danish border. The released prisoners then boarded a train to Copenhagen, complete with a large group of Danish police officers to protect them from Nazi soldiers. After the train arrived in Copenhagen, the women boarded a boat destined for Sweden.

When Jeannie finally felt safe, her body collapsed. Her unconscious body was rushed to the hospital, where she woke up to Swedish doctors taking care of her. At the time of her release, the frail woman only weighed about 70 pounds. She pleaded with one of her doctors to contact her parents and let them know that she was alive. The doctor simply told her that he did not want to get their hopes up. She had contracted tuberculosis during her time at the camp, and she would need a risky operation to get her back to health.

The operation was successful, but she had a long healing process ahead of her. She was sent to a hospital in the French mountains while she recuperated. While she was there, she met a brave and exceptional man. The man was Henri de Clarens, former bank manager and survivor of the Auschwitz and Buchenwald concentration camps. He was at the hospital being treated for his own injuries, and the two grew close during their time there.

9

JEANNIE'S LIFE AFTER THE WAR

World War II did not end for a few more months after Jeannie's release from the Ravensbruck camp. After returning home with a clean bill of health, Jeannie went about trying to live a normal life. Well, what she considered to be normal anyway. Henri, the man that she had met at the hospital, became her husband. Soon after, she gave birth to two children. She had a son, Pascal, and a daughter, Ariane.

She continued to work as an interpreter. However, this time she was not connected to any espionage ring or gathering information on the enemy. Instead, she was working freelance for the United Nations and some other international organizations. After she retired, she never spoke another word of German. However, the refusal did not stop her from enrolling both of her children in German language courses while they were in school.

She did her best to stay away from reporters and historians that wanted to hear her story. But, whether she liked it or not, the stories of her brilliant spy work and bravery were still being told. In 1993, veteran journalist Reginald Jones told the then CIA director James Woolsey about Jeannie's exploits and how she was a true example of what a real spy was supposed to be. Woolsey was moved by the stories that Jones told him and wanted to reward her for all of her hard work. She accepted the CIA's Agency Seal Medal, even though she still did not believe what she did was of any significance. With the award, the CIA stated that the award was "for brilliant and effective espionage, and for courage that is truly awe-inspiring" (Ignatius, 1998).

Jeannie Rousseau, who had been living in the shadows and enjoying the quiet life, showed up to the event to accept her medal in person. She stepped up to the microphone and in perfect English, she spoke to the American audience, "Perhaps it stirs us to think that if memory does not repeat itself, at least it stutters, and we might perhaps learn two or three little things from the past. Not from me, but perhaps through me" (Holmey, 2021).

For five more years, she stayed quiet about her work with the French Resistance, along with anything that had to do with the war. That is until she opened up to The Washington Post reporter, David Ignatius. By this time, she was 79-years-old, though she was still described as an alluring beauty. Her husband, Henri, had passed three years earlier, in 1995, and she spent most of her time enjoying the company of what was left of her family. Living in a small cottage on the Atlantic Coast in La Rochelle, France, she reluctantly told her story with her hoarse voice from years of heavy smoking. However, the journalist still spoke about how her eyes still held that certain sparkle that easily got the German soldiers to brag about their missions.

It was only after her interview with the journalist that Rousseau gained recognition in her own country. She went forward with an interview on a French radio broadcast, telling the same story that she had already told to Ignatius. That would be her last interview. Besides the two interviews that she agreed to participate in, there were two other people that she opened up to about what happened to her during the war– her children. It was a one-time occurrence, and a date was made as if it were a dinner reservation. The small family of four sat around the kitchen table and the children listened to their parents tell their stories. When asked if it was hard for her son and daughter to hear, she simply answered, "No. It was just hard for *them* to tell" (Ignatius, 1998).

She went on to tell the journalist the difference between Americans and the French, stating that the French did not celebrate suffering or their victimhood. "People wanted to forget. People did not want to know." (Ignatius, 1998). This seemed true for even the heroes of the war; they simply wanted to forget that it ever happened. Her story may have started off alluring, but there were parts that were just too painful to talk about.

Jeannie was asked many times why she did what she did. Why did she put her life in danger so many times when she could have stayed in Paris with everyone else? Why had she accepted Lamarque Georges' invitation to work with the Druids immediately when she could have easily said no? How did she manage to keep going, even when she thought she was going to die? Her answer, "I just did it, that's all. It was not a choice. It was what you did. At the time, we all thought we would die. I don't understand the question. How could I not do it?" (Ignatius, 1998).

CONCLUSION

In previous wars, women spies were usually used as a means of distraction. They were not normally sent out to gather information and oversee operations. When it came to the requirements for using women as spies, an officer for the Britain-based domestic-counterintelligence agency M15, Maxwell Knight, plainly stated that she would need to be "A clever woman who can use her personal attractions wisely". He also stated that the woman should not be one that was "oversexed or undersexed" (Mundy, 2019). His reasoning behind this statement? An undersexed woman would lack the charisma that would be needed to seduce her target. An oversexed woman would scare men away. That pretty much sums up the male perspective of what a quality female spy looked like: an attractive, charming, neutrally sexed woman that could type up reports while she batted her eyelashes and partook in pillow talk with the enemy.

This is what made the Second World War different from past wars. The demand for labor was high and left opportunities open for women to participate in the action. The United States went as far as creating a women's branch specifically for women, allowing them to partake in a field that had historically been dominated by men–espionage. With England leading the way with its formation of the SOE, women were recruited as spies and given jobs that were considered dangerous for a man.

Women were seen as less of a threat and could be given inconspicuous jobs where there was less of a chance of being suspected as a spy or being captured and interrogated. Many of the female spies traveled throughout France, working as wireless operators and couriers. Besides military intelligence agents, there were a number of women that worked alongside the French Resistance. The numerous women that joined in on the resistance movement engaged in the transportation of weapons and supplies, dangerous covert operations, and helping people escape from the threat of persecution.

The Nazi's traditional sexist beliefs made the women spies' jobs much easier. Their stereotypical views of women as domesticated females blinded them to the ability of a woman to be a spy or hold any significant positions above a housewife. Sexism amongst the ranks was also the reason that many of the female spies used code names. Aliases such as Jeannie Rousseau's "Amniarix" or Marie-Madeleine Fourcade's "Hedgehog" allowed them to hide their gender and made it more likely that they would be taken seriously within the male-dominated world of espionage.

While, in theory, Rousseau had used her good looks to distract the German soldiers, she had also used her wits to convince them to tell their secret plans. The men were left clueless and had no idea that she was a spy. Some of the soldiers were actually insulted the first time that Jeannie was arrested and accused of being a spy, even going so far as vouching for her. Then, when she met up with the same soldiers later in Paris, they still did not suspect her of any wrongdoing. If they had, she definitely would not have been invited out for drinks or to the German soldier parties on Avenue Hoche.

Using the talents that she already had, she used her ability to translate and speak German to gather information when she helped negotiate contracts with German occupiers. Her photographic memory made it easier to transmit the information, not relying on writing the information down where it could easily be found. Jeannie could simply look at the drawings and blueprints, then describe them later in perfect detail. She proved that women spies could be as cunning as their male counterparts, all while risking her life, withstanding torture at the concentration camps, and facing execution.

Jeannie was fearless as she headed into work every day, knowing that it could certainly be the day her cover was blown. She worked alongside the French Industrialists and spent much of her time meeting with high-ranking German officials at the Hotel Majestic. She may have relied on her good looks to get the men talking, but she used her solid work ethic to get herself into a position that would place her within "the lion's den." Using her girlish charm, she persuaded the German soldiers to think of her as one of their closest friends and confidantes. Many women spies did not make it six months without their cover being blown. Jeannie Rousseau made it four years before she was finally captured. However, as you may recall, she still managed to outsmart the guards, giving them her real name while knowing that her alias was on her camp assignment papers. She kept her cover, even while she was tortured for her escape from the *Königsberg* camp. Throughout the horrendous treatment that she endured in all three concentration camps, Rousseau never revealed that she was the one who gave the British forces stolen information regarding the V-2 launch sites. The woman that staged one of the greatest coups in World War II had been in the Nazi's possession the entire time, and they were none the wiser.

With everything she had been through, including her near-death experience after contracting tuberculosis, Jeannie still found the strength to keep the other women prisoners' hopes alive. The moment that she arrived at the camp, she told the other women at the camp about D-Day, how the Allied forces had their backs, and they would be saved soon. Knowing that there would be hell to pay when she got back to camp, Jeannie stood her ground and protested the women creating guns and ammunition that would ultimately help the Germans' war efforts. She created a census with as many names as she could gather and found a way to save them, not knowing if she would be alive by the time help showed up. Her selflessness was admirable, especially by today's standards.

In addition to receiving the CIA's Seal Medal she was honored many times for bravery. In 1955, 10 years after the war ended, she was made a member of France's Legion of Honor, the highest French Order of Merit that can be awarded to both military and civilian personnel. The Legion of Honor has within it five levels and in 2009 Jeannie's award was promoted to Grand Officer of the Legion, the second highest. However, two of the medals she earned were considered a slight towards her and other women spies. Although her reports on the planning, development, and location of the "V-weapons" were seen as one of the greatest coups of World War II, she was excluded from being awarded the *Compagnons de la Libération*, or Companions of Liberation, medal. Instead, she received the lesser honor, the Médaille de la Résistance, along with the *Croix de Guerre* award (Olson, 2019).

Jeannie's efforts in the espionage world have been called a "masterpiece of intelligence work". Even after all of the awards and all of the things that she went through, she is still considered to be one of the many forgotten female spies of World War II. She may not have thought what she did was very special, but the history buffs and the thousands of the people that she saved may beg to differ. The spy work that she performed proved on multiple occasions to be phenomenal and brave. She truly set herself apart from the rest in her field.

Ironically, the woman who used her gift of photographic memory to save so many people eventually succumbed to Alzheimer's disease. The German that she spoke so well that could have helped her pass for a German girl was forgotten in her old age. She would pass the house on Left Bank that she used to flee to after every German soldier party, but could not remember which one it was. Jeannie Rousseau died in Montaigu, Paris, on August 23, 2017, at the age of 98. She was survived by her two children and four grandchildren.

REFERENCES

Appraisal of U.S. Intelligence. (1996, February 23). *The Evolution of the U.S. Intelligence Community-An Historical Overview*. Irp.fas.org. https://irp.fas.org/offdocs/int022.html

BBC History. (2020, September 3). *Spying in WW2: how wartime espionage was just as dramatic as fiction*. HistoryExtra. https://www.histo ryextra.com/period/second-world-war/spying-espionage-ww2-wartime-reality-soe-mi5-mi6/

Binney, M. (2004). *The women who lived for danger : the women agents of SOE in the Second World War*. Coronet.

Boissoneault, L. (2017, November 9). *Was Vichy France a Puppet Government or a Willing Nazi Collaborator?* Smithsonian; Smithsonian.com. https://www.smithsonianmag.com/history/vichy-govern ment-france-world-war-ii-willingly-collaborated-nazis-180967160/

Bomboy, S. (2022, February 26). *How one telegram helped to lead America toward war* - National Constitution Center. National Constitution Center – Constitutioncenter.org. https://constitutioncenter.org/blog/how-one-telegram-helped-to-lead-america-toward-war

Brereton Greenhous, & Tattrie, J. (2018). *Battle of Amiens | World War I [1918]*. In Encyclopædia Britannica. https://www.britannica.com/event/Battle-of-Amiens

Britannica. (2019). *Dunkirk evacuation* | Facts, Pictures, & Summary. In Encyclopædia Britannica. https://www.britannica.com/event/Dunkirk-evacuation

Britannica. (2020). *Panzer* - Pz. IV. In Encyclopædia Britannica. https://www.britannica.com/technology/panzer/Pz-IV

Britannica. (2022a, March 16). *Battle of France - Aftermath of the Battle of France*. Encyclopedia Britannica. https://www.britannica.com/event/Battle-of-France-World-War-II/Aftermath-of-the-Battle-of-France

Britannica. (2022b, March 16). France - *German aggressions*. Encyclopedia Britannica. https://www.britannica.com/place/France/German-aggressions#ref465467

Britannica. (2021, October 8). *National Resistance Council | French history*. Encyclopedia Britannica. https://www.britannica.com/topic/National-Resistance-Council

Claire, M. (2016, January 13). *5 Reasons Why Women Make Great Spies*. Marie Claire. https://www.marieclaire.co.uk/life/work/5-reasons-why-women-make-great-spies-60754

Connelly, S. (2014, July 12). *New Yorker risks life as double agent in Nazi underground, brings down Duquesne Spy Ring: new book*. Nydailynews.com. https://www.nydailynews.com/news/world/new-yorker-risks-life-double-agent-nazi-underground-brings-duquesne-spy-ring-new-book-article-1.1864628

Deák, I. (2015). *Europe on trial : the story of collaboration, resistance, and retribution during World War II*. Westview Press.

Debruyne, E. (2014). *Espionage | International Encyclopedia of the First World War (WW1)*. 1914-1918-Online.net. https://encyclopedia.1914-1918-online.net/article/espionage

Donnell, C., & Spedaliere, D. (2017). *Maginot line gun turrets - and french gun turret development 1880-1940*. Bloomsbury Publishing Plc.

Dorling Kindersley Limited. (2022). *DK Find Out!* | Fun Facts for Kids on Animals, Earth, History and more! DK Find Out! https://www.dkfindout.com/uk/history/world-war-ii/french-resistance/

Ducksters. (2020). *Civil War: Spies*. Ducksters.com. https://www.ducksters.com/history/civil_war/spies.php

English Heritage. (2019). *Things you need to know about the Dunkirk Evacuation*. English Heritage. https://www.english-heritage.org.uk/visit/places/dover-castle/history-and-stories/operation-dynamo-things-you-need-to-know/

Evans, M. (2018). *A History of the French Resistance* | History Today. Historytoday.com. https://www.historytoday.com/reviews/history-french-resistance

FBI.gov. (2019). *Duquesne Spy Ring* | Federal Bureau of Investigation. Federal Bureau of Investigation. https://www.fbi.gov/history/famous-cases/duquesne-spy-ring

Gildea, R. (2017, September 6). *Jeannie Rousseau obituary.* The Guardian. https://www.theguardian.com/world/2017/sep/06/jeannie-rousseau-obituary

Gopnik, A. (2019). *How Charles de Gaulle Rescued France.* The New Yorker. https://www.newyorker.com/magazine/2018/08/20/how-charles-de-gaulle-rescued-france

Gruber, K. (2021, January 4). *Spies of the Revolutionary War.* American Battlefield Trust. https://www.battlefields.org/learn/articles/spies-revolutionary-war

Haynes, S. (2020, October 2). *Inside the Stories of the Most Daring Women Spies of World War II.* TIME. https://time.com/5892932/a-call-to-spy-real-history/

Herbert, U. (2004). *National-Socialist extermination policies : contemporary German perspectives and controversies.* Berghahn Books.

History. (2009, November 24). *Benedict Arnold commits treason.* HISTORY. https://www.history.com/this-day-in-history/benedict-arnold-commits-treason

History. (2018a, August 21). *France to surrender.* HISTORY. https://www.history.com/this-day-in-history/france-to-surrender

History. (2009a, November 9). *German-Soviet Nonaggression Pact.* HISTORY. https://www.history.com/topics/world-war-ii/german-soviet-nonaggression-pact#:~:text=On%20August%2023%2C%201939%E2%80%93shortly

History. (2009b, November 16). *Germany invades Poland.* HISTORY. https://www.history.com/this-day-in-history/germany-invades-poland#:~:text=On%20September%201%2C%201939%2C%20German

History. (2021, June 11). *Germany invades Paris.* History.com. https://www.history.com/this-day-in-history/germans-enter-paris#:~:text=On%20June%2014%2C%201940%2C%20Parisians

History. (2018b, August 21). Mata Hari executed. HISTORY. https://www.history.com/this-day-in-history/mata-hari-executed

Hitler, A. (1994). *Mein Kampf* (p. 526). Pimlico. (Original work published 1925)

Holmey, O. (2021, September 29). *Jeannie Rousseau, spy for the French Resistance.* The Independent. https://www.independent.co.uk/news/obituaries/jeannie-rousseau-spy-for-the-french-resistance-a7918426.html?fr=operanews

Holocaust Encyclopedia. (2021). *Oradour-sur-Glane.* Encyclopedia.ushmm.org. https://encyclopedia.ushmm.org/content/en/article/oradour-sur-glane

Holocaust Memorial Museum. (2019). *Public Humiliation.* Ushmm.org. https://encyclopedia.ushmm.org/content/en/article/public-humiliation

Ignatius, D. (1998, December 28). *AFTER FIVE DECADES, A SPY TELLS HER TALE.* Washington Post. https://www.washingtonpost.com/archive/politics/1998/12/28/after-five-decades-a-spy-tells-her-tale/8bfa5aae-5527-4eb5-8e45-878f1ec823fb/

Imperial War Museums. (2022). *Secret War: What you need to know.* Imperial War Museums. https://www.iwm.org.uk/history/secret-war-what-you-need-to-know

Intel.gov. (2021). *A New Nations First Spies.* Www.intelligence.gov. https://www.intelligence.gov/evolution-of-espionage/revolutionary-war/new-nations-first-spies

Intrado. (2022). *V for Victory Graffiti.* Www.wiltonnh.gov. https://www.wiltonnh.gov/about_wilton/interesting_places__hidden_in_plain_sight/v_for_victory_graffiti

Jackson, J. (2003). *France : the dark years, 1940-1944.* Oxford University Press.

Jones, R. V. (1978). *The Wizard War.* Coward, McCann & Geoghegan.

Kaiser, C. (2015, May 6). *What Americans forget about French resistance.* CNN. https://www.cnn.com/2015/05/06/opinions/kaiser-ve-day-french-resistance/index.html

Kindersley, D. (2019). *DK Find Out!* DK Find Out! https://www.dkfindout.com/us/history/world-war-i/spying-on-enemy/

Kitson, S. (2008). *The hunt for Nazi spies : fighting espionage in Vichy France (pp. 7–25).* University Of Chicago Press.

Kretaner, N. (2021, January 5). *French Armed Forces 1940*. WW2 Weapons. https://www.ww2-weapons.com/french-armed-forces-1940/

Lavergne, R. (2017, May 17). *France to shine light on men put to work on Hitler's secret weapon*. Www.timesofisrael.com. https://www.timesofisrael.com/france-to-shine-light-on-men-put-to-work-on-hitlers-secret-weapon/

Lehrer, S. (2013). *Compiègne*. Stevenlehrer.com. http://stevenlehrer.com/compiegne.htm

Lillian Goldman Law Library. (2008). *The Avalon Project : Franco-German Armistice : June 25, 1940*. Yale Law School. https://avalon.law.yale.edu/wwii/frgearm.asp

LRE Foundation. (2022). *The Liberation of Paris*. Www.liberationroute.com. https://www.liberationroute.com/stories/180/the-liberation-of-paris

McDermott, A. (2018, July 2). *How World War II Empowered Women*. HISTORY. https://www.history.com/news/how-world-war-ii-empowered-women#:~:text=World%20War%20II%20mobiliza tion%20affected

McFadden, C. (2017, March 25). *Hitler's Doomed Schwerer Gustav: Largest Gun Mankind Has Ever Built*. Interestingengineering.com. https://interestingengineering.com/schwerer-gustav-the-biggest-cannon-during-wwii

Merriam-Webster Dictionary. (n.d.). *Definition of SPY*. Www.merriam-Webster.com. Retrieved March 27, 2022, from https://www.merriam-webster.com/dictionary/spy

Mizokami, K. (2018, October 6). *The StG-44: Nazi Germany's Assault Rifle That Help Inspire the M4 Carbine*. The National Interest. https:// nationalinterest.org/blog/buzz/stg-44-nazi-germanys-assault-rifle-help-inspire-m4-carbine-32847

Morris, N. (2011, February 17). *BBC - History - World Wars: The Special Operations Executive 1940 - 1946*. Www.bbc.co.uk. https:// www.bbc.co.uk/history/worldwars/wwtwo/soe_01.shtml#:~: text=On%20July%2016%2C%201940%2C%20Prime

Moure, K. (2010). *Food Rationing and the Black Market in France (1940-1944)*. French History, 24(2), 262–282. https://doi.org/10.1093/ fh/crq025

Mundy, L. (2017, December 28). *Jeannie Rousseau de Clarens: The Glass Ceiling-Breaking Spy*. POLITICO Magazine. https://www. politico.com/magazine/story/2017/12/28/jeannie-rousseau-de-clarens-obituary-216181/

Mundy, L. (2019, May 12). *World War II's Female Spies and Their Secrets*. The Atlantic; The Atlantic. https://www.theatlantic.com/ magazine/archive/2019/06/female-spies-world-war-ii/588058/

NMAF. (2022). *Messerschmitt Me 262A Schwalbe*. National Museum of the United States Air Force. https://www.nationalmuseum.af.mil/ Visit/Museum-Exhibits/Fact-Sheets/Display/Article/196266/ messerschmitt-me-262a-schwalbe/

OCCHINO, F., OOSTERLINCK, K., & WHITE, E. N. (2008). *How Much Can a Victor Force the Vanquished to Pay? France under the Nazi Boot*. The Journal of Economic History, 68(1), 1–45. https://doi. org/10.1017/s0022050708000016

Olson, L. (2019). *Madame Fourcade's secret war : the daring young woman who led France's largest spy network against Hitler.* Random House.

Paxton, R. O. (2001). *Vichy France : old guard and new order, 1940-1944.* Columbia University Press.

Peck, M. (2017, March 4). *Mexico Almost Invaded the U.S. in 1917.* The National Interest. https://nationalinterest.org/blog/the-buzz/mexico-almost-invaded-the-us-1917-19663

Pickles, D. M. (2019). *Charles de Gaulle* | Biography, World War II, & Facts. In Encyclopædia Britannica. https://www.britannica.com/biography/Charles-de-Gaulle-president-of-France

Popowycz, J. (2021, December 22). *Warsaw Burning: The German Response to the Warsaw Uprising.* The National WWII Museum | New Orleans. https://www.nationalww2museum.org/war/articles/german-response-warsaw-uprising

Robuck, E. (2021, April 2). *Five Fearless Female WWII Spies and Resistors.* CrimeReads. https://crimereads.com/five-fearless-female-wwii-spies-and-resistors/

Rosbottom, R. C. (2015). *When Paris went dark : the City of Light under German occupation, 1940-44.* John Murray.

Savage, D. (2022, March 10). *Women Who Risked Everything: Female Spies of World War II.* Www.lapl.org. https://www.lapl.org/collections-resources/blogs/lapl/women-who-risked-everything-female-spies-world-war-two#:~:text=They%20bravely%20engaged%20in%20covert

SciencesPo. (2018, September 5). *The Spy Who Studied at Sciences Po.* Sciences Po. https://www.sciencespo.fr/en/news/news/the-spy-who-studied-at-sciences-po/3748

Sebba, A. (2017). *Les Parisiennes : how the women of Paris lived, loved and died in the 1940s.* London Weidenfeld & Nicolson.

Sheldon, N. (2017, June 1). *Fearless Females: 10 Resistance Fighters from World War I & II You Might Not heard of.* HistoryCollection.com. https://historycollection.com/ten-fearless-female-resistance-fighters-first-second-world-wars/3/

Shepherd, B. (2016). *Hitler's soldiers : the German army in the Third Reich.* Yale University Press.

Simkin, J. (1997, September). *French Army.* Spartacus Educational. https://spartacus-educational.com/2wwfrenchA.htm

Simkin, J. (1997, September). *Paul Reynaud.* Spartacus Educational. https://spartacus-educational.com/2WWreynaud.htm

Smith, A. (2019, April 16). *Women Spies During WWII Were Way Better At Keeping Secrets Than Their Male Counterparts.* CrimeReads. https://crimereads.com/women-spies-during-wwii-were-way-better-at-keeping-secrets-than-their-male-counterparts/

Specktor, B. (2020, March 10). *Long-lost bunker belonging to "Churchill's secret army" discovered in Scottish forest.* Livescience.com. https://www.livescience.com/secret-auxiliary-unit-bunker.html

The Guardian. (2009, September 8). *Life in occupied France during the second world war.* The Guardian; The Guardian. https://www.theguardian.com/world/2009/sep/08/life-in-occupied-france-nazi

United States Holocaust Memorial Museum. (2019). *Deceiving the Public*. Ushmm.org. https://encyclopedia.ushmm.org/content/en/article/deceiving-the-public

Vinen, R. (2006). *The unfree French : life under the occupation*. Yale University Press.

Walsh, B. (n.d.). *The National Archives Learning Curve | The Great War | Why was it hard to make peace?* Www.nationalarchives.gov.uk. Retrieved April 1, 2022, from https://www.nationalarchives.gov.uk/education/greatwar/g5/cs2/background.htm#:~:text=The%20German%20army%20was%20limited

Weiner, T. (1993, August 11). *U.S. Spied on Its World War II Allies*. The New York Times. https://www.nytimes.com/1993/08/11/world/us-spied-on-its-world-war-ii-allies.html

ABOUT THE AUTHOR

Jo has a love of history and a fascination of how it has shaped the present. She grew up in rural America alongside her three elder brothers. Her maternal Grandmother (Mémé), with whom she was very close, emigrated to the US from France, post WWII. It was not until near the end of Mémé's life that she spoke to Jo about the war years. She described these years as being full of incredible hardship and loss but also of courage and great friendships. Moved by these stories of bravery, determination and fellowship, Jo began writing stories about inspirational young men and women during her high school years.

Jo lives in Maryland with her husband, their three children and two Maine Coon cats. She has travelled extensively through Europe and the US and loves to explore the history of new places. She also enjoys walking on the beach, gardening, playing chess and listening to music.